ba   uran

designs

Outstanding bar and restaurant designs

THE ARTS OF THE HABITAT

Series directed by Olivier Boissière

Front cover
Kabuto.
A restaurant whose decor
evokes an Italo-Japanese film.

Back cover
Torres de Avila.
The Moon Tower bar,
like a magical universe seen
in a dream.

Preceding page
Barna Crossing,
Fukuoka, Japan.
The nightclub as imagined by
Alfredo Arribas–somewhere
between a pleasure garden
and a hypertecch sound and
light show.

Publisher editor: Jean-François Gonthier
Art director: Bruno Leprince
Cover design: Daniel Guerrier
Editing staff: Olivier Boissière, Olivier de Vleeschouwer, Martine Colombet
Translation: Rubye Monet
Assistant to the publisher: Sophie-Charlotte Legendre
Correction and revision: Jack Monet
Composition: Graffic, Paris
Filmsetting: Compo Rive Gauche, Paris
Lithography: ARCO Editorial, Barcelone

This edition copyright © TELLERI, PARIS 1998
All illustrations copyright © ARCO Editorial except for the cover
ISBN : 2-7450-0011-X
Printed in Italy

Contents

Introduction

In the mid-1960s, the great Milton Glaser, designer, illustrator and graphic artist, was writing a column for a trendy New York magazine. It was called "Food and Mood" and in it the appreciation of the gastronomy was accompanied by comments on the decor and ambience of the place.

A sign of the times, perhaps. For the old turn-of-the-century setting, where the rites of fine dining were carried out in pomp and decorum in accordance with the aesthetics of the day, seemed finally a thing of the past. While waiting for an Aalto to conceive another Savoye or a Johnson another Four Seasons, we turned out endless copies of Art Deco brasseries or reproduced Louis-Philippe interiors.

Then, from the depths of the night came the Renaissance, with the Main Bleue by Philip Starck and the Roter Engel by Coop Himmelblau.

For the new generation bored by Sunday dinners in old family restaurants, a new type of dining/drinking place came into being: insolent, intentionally noisy and colorful, an integral part of the new culture, and of which it has assimilated all the outward signs. Theme restaurants, places that take their cue from the recognition of and adhesion to the themes of popular myth: music (the Hard Rock Cafés), cinema (Planet Hollywood), even star models (Fashion Café).

On a more ceremonious note, Starck (once again) invented the restaurant with a strangely theatrical air, where the guest was both actor and spectator and the feeling was one of eerie rituals in a decor as stunning as it was subtle. At the same time he gave the rest rooms an ironic dignity and new sociability, where one could exchange gossip, addresses or eloquent come-ons.

With the growing internationalism of our shrinking planet, café-society has become more cosmopolitan. It has also become more demanding with respect to the appearance of its dining places and pleasure domes. Bars, restaurants and night clubs have gained in originality, while sharing the same signs and references. The nomads of design who exercise their talents today in London or Tokyo, tomorrow in Los Angeles or Stockholm, have understood that these ephemeral places are transitory yet necessary—and the design they practice is a fertile intermingling of styles and of cultures.

The collection "Cafés, Bars and Restaurants" presents a selection of the gay and playful designs that have sprung up in all the capitals of the world. They form a brilliant kaleidoscope attracting the social set of the moment in a whirlwind of excitement and frivolity, where the wit and fantasy of architects and designers find free expression.

La Gare, Milan.
Un espace en désuétude réinsvesti par le monde de la nuit. Des objets colorés et spectaculaires effacent la structure originelle.

The People's Palace, Royal Festival Hall
London, Great Britain

From the entrance,
the first impression
is one of precision
and sobriety in the
treatment of details—
brightly-colored shapes
against a white wall
frame the wooden door
of the cloakroom.

Opposite:
The facelift carried out
by Allies and Morrison
has transformed
an ungainly space into
a luminous and inviting
restaurant. They have
truly lured the people
back to the "people's
palace."

New York's MOMA and Amsterdam's Stedelijk Museum were undoubtedly the first major cultural sites to offer their visitors decent restaurant facilities, a choice that in no way reduced their charm. Following their example, other cultural institutions gradually overcame their aversion to going from "sublime to ridiculous," i.e., combining their treasures of art, music or theater with more mundane considerations of the restaurant/snack bar/tea room variety. Business is, after all, business.

The Royal Festival Hall is a venerable institution born of the Festival of Great Britain, the great exhibition that ran from 1949 to 1951. The Hall, its only surviving building, was used as a theater and concert hall. The complex was enlarged in 1964 to include galleries and a restaurant, and again in 1968, when two new facilities were added: a concert hall dedicated to the Queen and an edifice devoted to the plastic arts, the Hayward Gallery. All the parts were linked by pedestrian walkways in the "brutalist" taste of the day. The restaurants, never very attractive, closed in 1992. The South Bank of the Thames seemed to be in the direst of straits.

The whole complex was badly in need of a facelift, especially in view of the fact that it was in the very heart of the future development projects for the area. It was felt that the creation of new restaurants would help change the

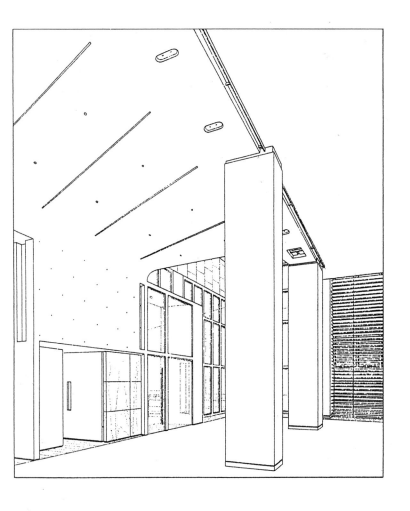

Perspective drawings
of the restaurant
interior and of
the entrance, showing
the access walkway.

Ground plan.

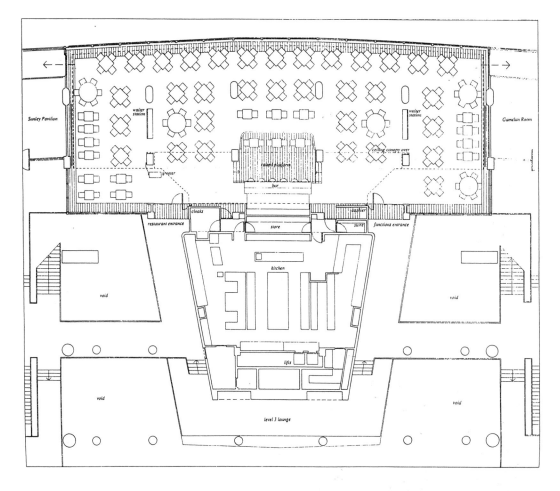

image of the entire site, and the task of designing them was given to the architects Allies and Morrison. A short-lived structure in the Hayward Gallery reopened in 1994 and the restaurant for the complex itself was dubbed the People's Palace.

The People's Palace occupies a vast space on three levels between the foyer and the auditorium of the Royal Festival Hall, and enjoys a panoramic view over the Thames. In the central core the architects placed the kitchen and utility rooms, with a long travertine-covered bar running up against it and an entrance to the restaurant on either side. The entire space, from top to bottom, is broken up into parallel bands by the massive pillars that support the auditorium. Making of necessity a virtue, the architects have used this constraint to the best advantage. They have placed the tables in rows parallel to the river, assuring the best possible views. A broad canopy of stucco, reinforced with glass wool, with a shape that resembles the interiors of Finnish architect Alvar Aalto, dissimulates the underside of the auditorium, giving the space a roundness it lacked and transforming an awkward area into a large inviting dining place. Blond wood furniture, seat coverings in pale gray, soft lighting, windows hung with venetian blinds and punctuated by light fixtures, all combine to create an atmosphere of quiet and gentleness. People are now flocking to the People's Palace.

Blond wood accentuates the luminosity created by the white-painted surfaces and large windows that soar to the full height of the room.
The bar, slightly raised on a wooden platform, and a group of tables placed nearby.

The great volume of the restaurant is broken up by the massive verticals of the pillars that support the auditorium.

Against the wall that
separates the kitchen
and utilities from the
restaurant proper, the bar
—covered in travertine
the same shade as the
carpeting—occupies a
central position between
the two access areas.

The tables placed
parallel to the windows
and running the whole
length of the restaurant
seem to expand the
space while offering
a panoramic view of
the Thames.

The access to the
People's Palace from
the staircase linking the
vestibule of Royal
Festival Hall to the
auditorium—the entire
ensemble radiates a
geometry of light.

The wall separating
the restaurant from
the kitchen curves
upward in a great
wavelike movement
that tempers the
strong verticals of the
pillars.

Cafeteria of the Fine Arts Museum

Vienna, Austria

Nowadays, our museums boast riches beyond the paintings and sculptures they possess. For some years now, they have taken to equipping themselves with cafeterias, places that may have little to do with the collections per se but that offer visitors the comfort and well-being needed to create a favorable atmosphere for enjoying their collections. These new cafeterias have revolutionized some of the world's principle museums, whose curators had until then been so focused on the genius of dead artists that they had forgotten that museums are frequented by men and women who, sensitive though they may be to spiritual nourishment, have not for all that given up the pleasures of food and drink.

In a growing number of museums, often as vast as railroad stations (there, at least, the traveler's appetite was never overlooked) these cafeterias have flourished, providing a welcome rest for a tired public during its (one hopes) culturally fruitful tour.

Thus, a major preoccupation of many museum directors over the past few decades has been to get rid of the existing facilities, where you could often hope for no better than a bad cup of coffee in a cramped or drafty corner, and create entirely new spaces where it would not be forbidden for the user to feel comfortably settled. When Vienna's Fine Arts Museum was about to undergo a general renovation, the decision was made to incorporate a cafeteria.

The Museum had been built between 1872 and 1881 by Gottfried Semper and Karl Hasenauer, and the latter was also responsible for the interior design of great artistic value. The project of creating the cafeteria, given to the Austrian architect Gert M. Mayr-Keber, involved integrating it perfectly into this prestigious space. The first floor hallway was immediately chosen as the site. What now remained was to compose the design.

Mayr-Keber, a graduate of the Technical University of Vienna, had set up his own agency in 1979. A professor at Vienna's University of Applied Arts, he was also a visiting professor at the State Academy of Visual Arts in Stuttgart and taught at the Technical University of Vienna.

Aside from the purely aesthetic aspect of visual integration already mentioned, he had to reflect on the problems of lighting and acoustics—the best way to install artificial lighting and provide soundproofing. The thin metallic structure that holds the lighting took its inspiration from classic crystal chandeliers. From this support, low-voltage halogen lamps diffuse a discrete and muted light. Practically invisible in the general architectural organization, this structure reduces to a minimum

Opposite:

Set in the large vestibule on the first floor of the museum, the cafeteria has been integrated with lightness and finesse into the prestigious interior designed by Karl Hasenauer in the latter half of the 19th century. Under the ornate arcades of gilded marble, a metallic network of spiderweb delicacy holds the suspended light fixtures, whose points of contact with the structure have been kept to a minimum.

Ground plan showing the geometric
patterns of the marble floors and the
placement of the tables in the
cafeteria.

Opposite:
Around the central area with its
circular bar, the large peripheral
galleries provide a vast and restful
space where nothing shocks the eye.
The furniture, all in black and white,
consists of comfortable cloth-covered
armchairs in an irregular geometric
print and tables on a slim metal base.
The overall effect is sober, well-
matched and very Viennese.

the points of contact with the original environment. When this contact was unavoidable, it was done in such a way as to be practically imperceptible. Elements of construction and ornamentation were conceived along the same criteria of lightness and weightlessness, so that the ensemble seems to float above the ground and the cafeteria seems all the more spacious as there is nothing to crush the perspective.

The water installation also posed a problem since there were no existing canalizations and new pipes had to laid. It was decided that no attempt should be made to camouflage these pipes, but rather to let them show and even in some cases to make their path coincide with the ornamental geometry of the marble floor. The fabric for the furniture was chosen with the same aim—something that would go well in the marble surroundings. Black and white, it echoes elements of the floor and permits the comfortable armchairs to blend right in.

An integral part of the museum, the cafeteria does not in any way affect the visual equilibrium. It exists completely, never seeking to hide itself yet never distracting the eye from the imposing presence of marble columns or stairways. The Austrian architect has succeeded in the task of beautifully integrating a warm and intimate space into a monumental decor.

Alfredo Arribas

Schirn Café, Kunsthalle

Frankfurt-am-Main, Germany

Opposite:

In the heart of the
Kunsthalle, and
accessible directly from
the street, a vast and
luminous space where
the exuberant Catalan
architect Alfredo
Arribas has conceived
a design quieter than
his usual register.
The bar, in the shape of
a widened horseshoe,
is the master element
around which the space
is organized.

Blond wood, off-white
and a pearl-like pale
gray—a color scheme
that is gentle, sober
and serene.

View behind the bar,
done completely
in stainless steel.

A striking feature of our era (that not all have greeted with approval) will have been to broaden the notion of culture, making it accessible to the greatest number. This highly commendable objective of democratization was accompanied by a host of spinoff products. Nowhere in the world today (at least nowhere in the Western world) is there a single museum worthy of the name that does not have its gift shop where the visitor can purchase the souvenir of his choice, be it a cultural gadget, a designer object, a T-shirt in the latest "in colors" or merely a catalogue. Besides these shops, the cultural engineers have not neglected to provide sites for our earthly nourishment as well, timidly at first, then with greater assurance.

The Frankfurt Kunsthalle (an art gallery with no permanent collection) particularly stands out in this respect. Devoted entirely to temporary exhibitions, its cafe, brasserie and snack bar give it a kind of continuity, a permanence in time. Frankfurt-am-Main is Germany's most active business center. In recent decades the greatest architects have been called upon to create the buildings that have added to its image of

Computer drawing
showing a general
perspective of the
building.

General plan of the bar,
restaurant and
cafeteria.

Longitudinal cross-
section showing the Art
Center's three levels.

Opposite:
At the rear of the room
a long bench of ivory-
colored leather follows
the curved wall of
the facade. The tables
in the cafeteria receive
natural light through
a double row of tall
vertical windows.

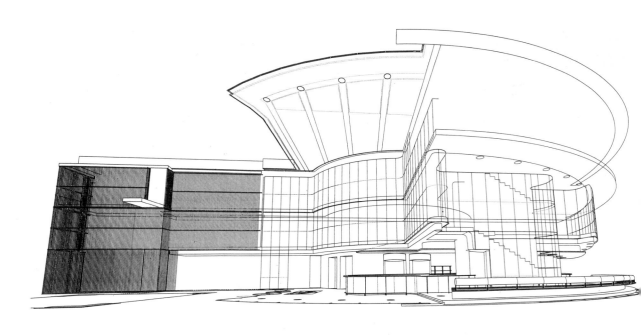

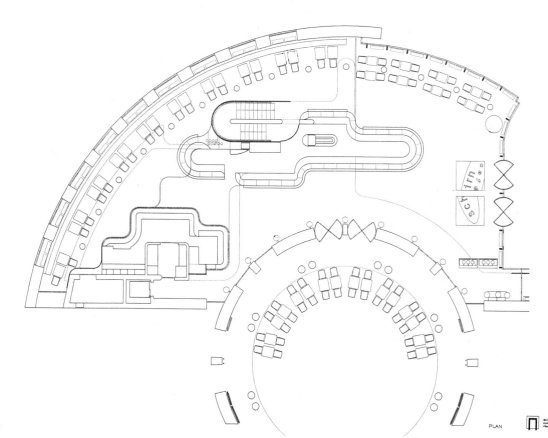

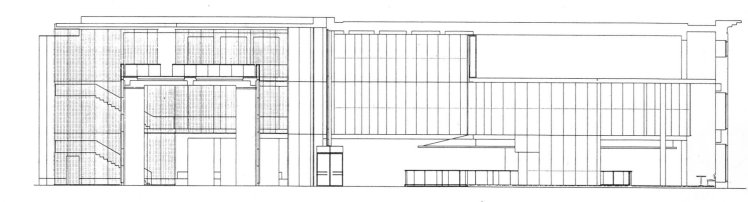

The long bar seems to stretch endlessly toward the cylindrical form of the revolving door.

The slightly rounded horizontal of the false ceiling provides a counterpoint to the strong verticals of the broad windows, which frame the tower of Saint-Bartholemew's Cathedral.

26 Schirn Café, Frankfurt-am-Main, Germany

an international city: Sir Norman Foster, Helmut Jahn and Richard Meier, to name but three, all completed prestigious works there. It stands to reason that the Kunsthalle would call upon a designer of renown to design its eating-place and bring it a cosmopolitan touch. Still, the choice of Alfredo Arribas was a surprising one. A leading figure of the *Interiorismo* movement that developed in Barcelona in the 1980s, Arribas was known for his baroque, exuberant and colorful realizations, bars and discos aglitter with glaring lights. With the Schirn Café, he shows his versatility and his ability to treat with equal talent a place that is relaxed but dignified, in tune with the art of the day. Situated on the ground floor of the Kunsthalle, the Schirn Café has two separate entrances, one directly onto the street, ·the other accessible from the exhibition space. Thus, the café functions independently of the exhibition schedule.

The space given over to the Schirn Café is complex in dimension and presents strong constraints—a segment of a cylinder, with ceilings of three different heights, a line of pillars just inside the front windows, a staircase to the upper floor placed, as if by chance, in the middle of the room. Arribas has managed to draw all the best from these constraints, to use the apparent disorder to his advantage. He has created two strong objects on a scale with the place—the kitchen, which he sets against one wall and which provides a round and opaque volume with a surface of stainless steel, and the bar in the shape of a widened horseshoe that creates two parallel circulations from the street entrance. All in blond wood, its supple fluid lines are accentuated by a false ceiling suspended over it, which follows its contours and takes in the staircase in one and the same movement.

Placed in a line along the rounded facade, the tables are set in a clear pattern, rhythmically punctuated by the pillars.

Arribas has made the best use of the resources by moderating the different heights and by opposing long supple horizontals to the strong verticals of the facade woodwork. A chromatic scale of gentle colors, mainly steel and various wood tones, and a soft, restrained look, without any of the brusque and startling traits that once made his style, show the great Catalan designer in a new light. With the Schirn Café, Arribas demonstrates his ability to solve a delicate problem in a subtle manner, with full respect for the spirit of the place.

An island of bottles encircled by the sinuous curve of the bar.

Opposite:
The suspended false ceiling, which incorporates the staircase leading to the Kunsthalle's upper level, follows and echoes the winding lines of the bar. It is also functional, containing the lighting and cooling fixtures.

Kristian Gavoille
Café Gavoille
Amiens, France

Opposite:
To see and be seen...
Inspired by the painting
"Nighthawks,"
by Edward Hopper,
the broad brightly-lit
windows are
an invitation to all birds
of the night to enter.

Behind the bar,
the oversized bottle-
rack with its strange
pagoda-like air.

Curiously playful
typography, with the
name that seems to be
handwritten on the
door, as an artist puts
his signature at the
bottom of a painting.

The city of Amiens, in northern France, was rebuilt after the war by Auguste Perret, the grand old man of modern French architecture. In the early 1970s, in line with the policy launched by Culture Minister André Malraux, Amiens was given a new state cultural center, the Maison de la Culture. By the 1990s the facilities had aged and the initial concept had to be revised to suit a new vision of culture (less solemn and also more profitable). As part of the rehabilitation of the theater, it was decided to add a restaurant that would be open to the street. The project was put in the hands of Kristian Gavoille.

Gavoille makes no secret of his long collaboration with the great French designer Philippe Starck, from whom he has inherited both a strong professionalism and an absence of modesty. Naming a public establishment after oneself (or at least allowing it to be so named) implies a good dose of narcissism, not to say pure cheek, two qualities that Starck has in abundance. More convincing, though, is the ability to give a place a strong sense of theatricality. The street facade of the Café Gavoille is a deliberate allusion to the

Seen from the street, the
building, dating from the 1960s,
has a distinct resemblance
to a service station.

The wash basin and the strange
object holding the faucet are
treated in a sculptural manner.

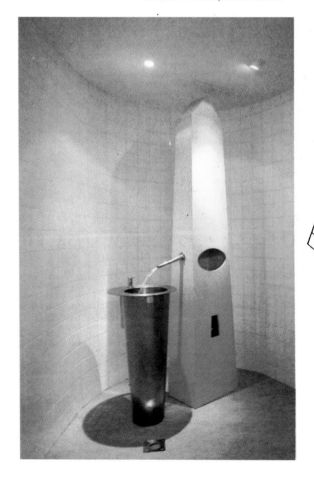

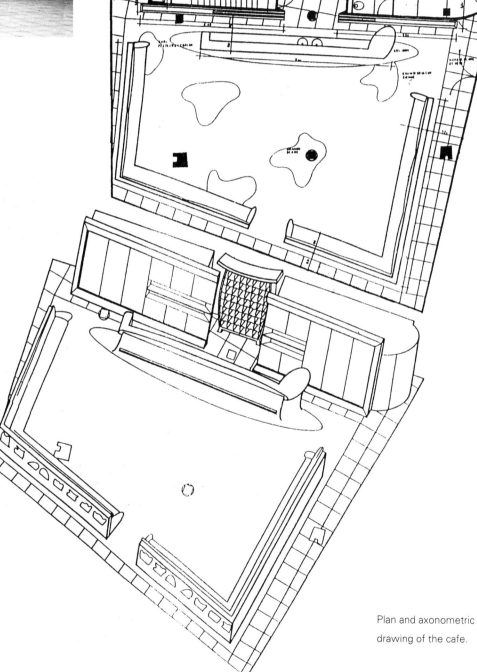

Plan and axonometric
drawing of the cafe.

A fleeting reference
to classicism, the
marble bar top ends
with a volute,
like an Ionic column.

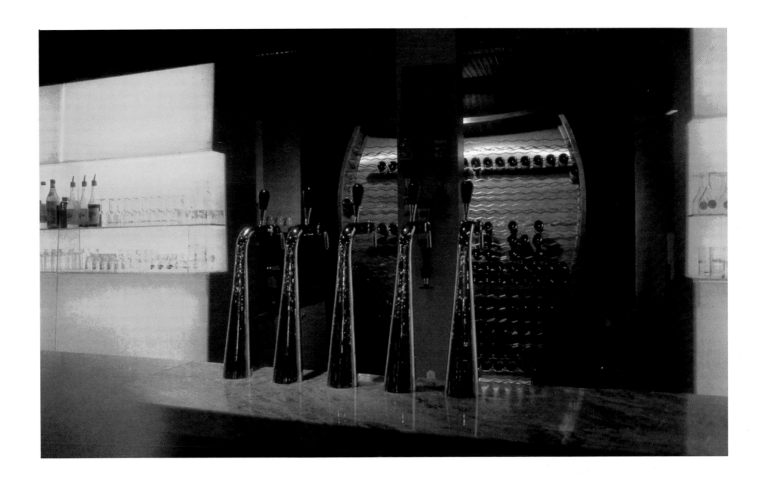

Myriad relections on
the dazzling stainless
steel of the beer taps
look like thousands
of effervescent golden
bubbles.

The master structure
of the entire scene,
a luminous screen
of frosted glass behind
the bar.

famous Edward Hopper painting "Nighthawks." The night-hawks of the painting are seen through a plate glass cafe window under a stark light that infuses the setting with solitude and gloom. Here this danger is avoided. Despite the broad facade on the street, the two L-shaped benches detached from the front and turned inward make the bar the focal point of the place.

The bar is 11 meters (36 feet) long, with a dark walnut base and a countertop of marble, whose scroll-like ends give it a touch of fantasy in classic style. In the center, a curious object of stainless steel, shaped strangely like an Oriental pagoda, serves as a bottle rack.

Two elements of the original structure have been included in the decor—from the bare ceiling of honeycombed concrete, Gavoille has hung two crystal chandeliers (an homage to the theaters of the past century) that have no light of their own but function by reflecting the many spots placed in their immediate proximity; the square pillars he has turned into graphic supports (like the striking "OUI") with a few coat hooks attached here and there at random.

Gavoille has designed all the furniture for his café. The design is sober—a gray metal base, gray-flecked laminated plastic for the stool and table tops, and for the seats, molded plastic shells covered with colored fabric.

Just like Starck, he gives the restrooms the attention they deserve. Against a light-colored background emerge two specific objects: one a stainless steel basin on a cone-like base, the other a multifunctional obelisk combining waste-basket, faucets and hand-dryer, under the woodwork of pale birds-eye elm, mute witness of our nightly ablutions.

Unlike the lonely setting in the painting, the bar at one end takes the form of a round table, well-suited to friendly group conversation.

Study for a stool. The colors and materials match those of the tables.

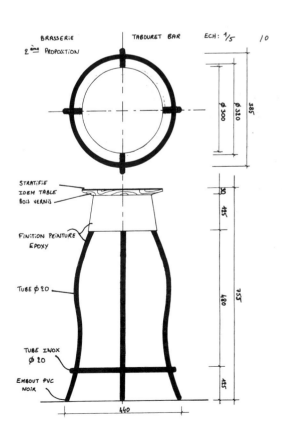

The L-shaped booths form an inner perimeter focused around the bar. The mute, heavy pillars of the original structure have been made eloquent by an application of words.

Suspended from the coffered ceiling, the crystal chandeliers shine with a soft glow, reflecting, like the moon, the light of the surrounding spots.

With its acid colors and highlights of brightest red, the lighting helps to anchor the space in the night and pays homage to a sound-stage or theater set.

Taxim Nightpark
Istanbul, Turkey

Outside, a neo-punk aesthetic: the outer shell of the old factory building was deliberately kept in its former state of dilapidation. The frosted glass of the set-back windows shows traditional motifs taken from Turkish textiles.

Opposite:
Inside, a second skin transfigures the space and softens the brutality of the structure. The restaurant boasts some luxurious touches: against the rear wall, "the longest leather canape in the world."

There is hardly a city in the Western world today that does not boast its trendy night spot combining restaurants, bars and dancing places in a single site, and where the youth of today rediscover (though they may not know it) a new version of the old unities of classical drama—the unities of space, time and action with, however, less dramatic effects.

Turkey stands at the gates of Europe. Beloved by the Americans who see in it a bulwark against the unpredictable East, Turkey has slowly been adopting Western ways. A case in point: the Taxim Nightpark, a vast nightclub along the now familiar and acceptable lines of cosmopolitan café society, founded by a young Turkish entrepreneur. Installed in a dis-affected factory building, Taxim Nightpark would not look out of place in London, Tokyo or New York.

Indeed, when it came to the interior design, the developer, Metin Fadillioglu, called upon one of the most nomadic of architectural firms, Branson and Coates, who work simultane-ously out of London, Tokyo and Milan and who are very much a part of the jet set of modern design.

A nightclub of this type has certain strong and constant constraints: there are stringent norms of fire safety to be followed, the air conditioning apparatus is over-sized and the

Immediate boarding: a metal gangway, like that of an air terminal, leads from the restaurant to the discotheque.

In the basement restrooms: tiling and white basins, chrome faucets and accessories overlapping the mirrors, mottled paint, all bathed in a cold harsh light.

Opposite:
Between the restaurant and the gangway to the discotheque, "the longest bead curtain in the world" repeats on a large scale the traditional motif of the eye.

Branson and Coates have integrated
several works by contemporary artists
into the decor. In the first-floor sofa room,
a mural by Stuart Helm dialogues
with classic motifs from Turkish textiles.

sound system must be capable of producing an impressive number of decibels.

Internal circulation must be fluid while access from the outside is strictly controlled by a skilled physionomist assisted by a team of hefty and unsmiling bouncers. For the rest, the architects can give free rein to all their fantasy. The only commandment is: "Astonish us!"

Branson and Coates have obeyed the laws of the genre, and cunningly mixed ingredients from three different sets of images. First, those of the world of work—the outer shell of the factory has been kept in its former state of dilapidation, the spirit of which is not so much that of industrial archeology as a kind of "No future" look, an extension of "punk" aesthetics. The interior, which looks as if it had been vitrified by a sudden blast of global warming, serves as an envelope for the new interior design. The "box within a box" bears literal signs of the world of international air travel: walkways and passages like those in an airline terminal, colored signposts and blinking, spinning, constantly shifting lights make up the decor of the vast discotheque. Large cargo containers serve as booths for video projections. The role of Turkish Airlines in all this remains a mystery. Are they merely contributors or did they participate in the whole project? For a touch of local color, a reference to vernacular culture, the various windows and mirrors that separate the different areas have been decorated with motifs from Turkish folklore. This mix of genres, this shish-kebab of design, projects a three-in-one atmosphere that cannot fail to inspire ambiguous feelings in the user. From the dance floor, with its airs of airport runway, to the bar, furnished with overstuffed divans that dimly evoke the oriental seraglio, Taxim Nightpark winks at us as if to say: mysterious East or inscrutable West...?

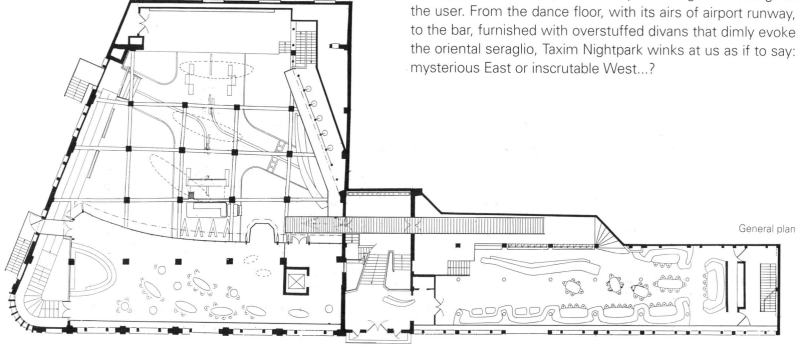

General plan

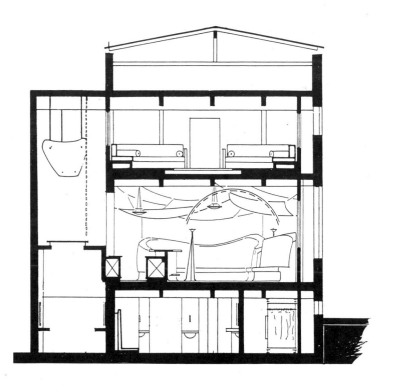

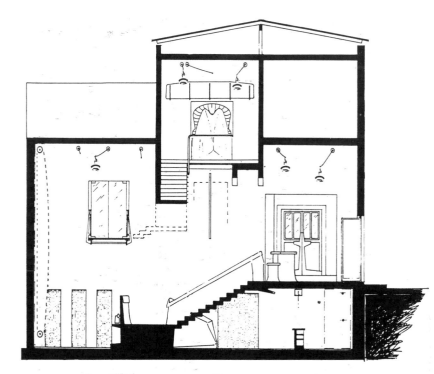

Vertical section of both
ends of the building.

Longitudinal section.

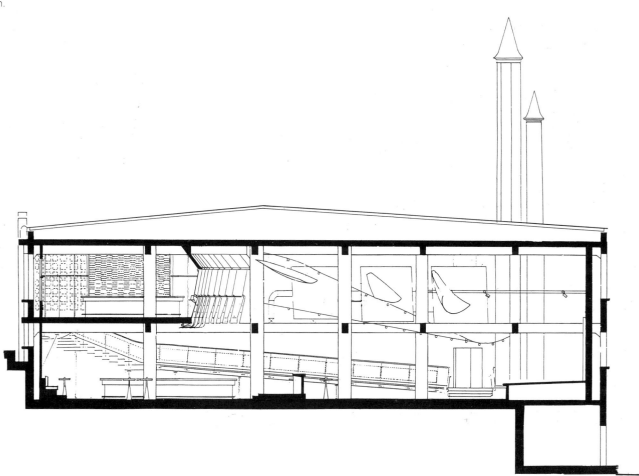

The vast discotheque,
a sort of airport runway
where the play of
colored lights imparts
a feeling of perpetual
motion. The aeronautic
theme is repeated
and conjugated with
emblematic signs of
Istanbul in a large
painting by Nigel Coates.

Opposite:
Between the various
levels of the building,
staircases and
gangways are
impeccably worked into
a rough decor,
fragments of which
have been deliberately
preserved in their
former state.

Detail of the utility area:
a mixture of dull pastel
tones and peeling
surfaces of the old
pillars.

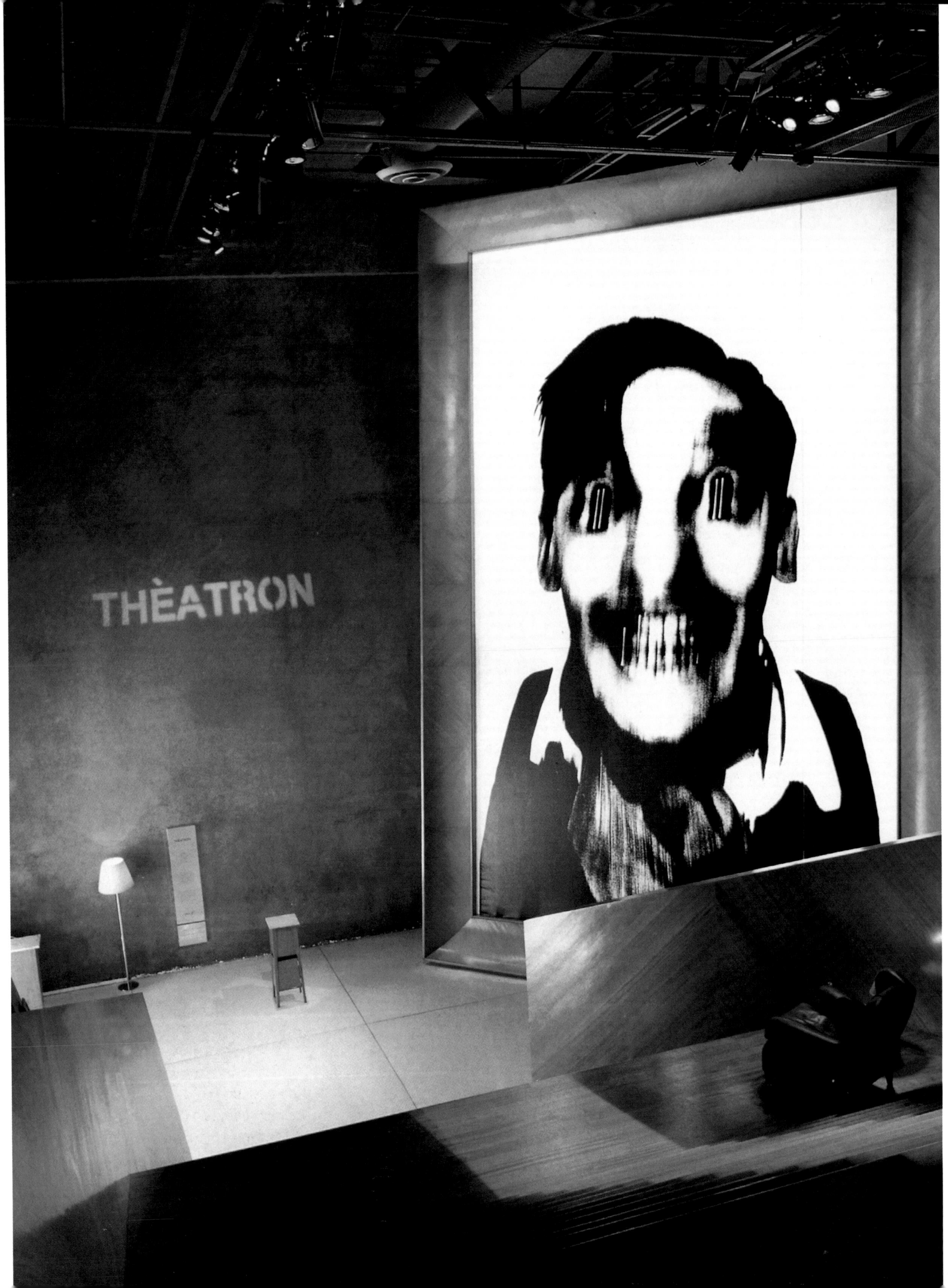
THÈATRON

Thèatron

Mexico City, Mexico

Mixing registers: a
boutique where bottles
of liquor and designer
objects are displayed
side by side in glass
cases or on pedestals,
in the manner
of a museum.

Opposite:
One enters the
Theatron via what
was once the stage,
whose entire height
the architect has
preserved. Over this
enormous space
towers a huge blow-up
of a grinning head by
photographer Richard
Avedon.

Philip Starck is undoubtedly one of the most prolific creators of our era. Objects, furniture, interiors, architecture, nothing has escaped the vivacity of his look or his bottomless creativity. Rising from out of the Paris nights, well-attuned to the changing sensibilities of the time, Starck has renewed the vision of an entire generation. In the area of hotel, cafe and restaurant design, he has shown himself to be a constant innovator. In his own provocative way he has updated the laws of hospitality. With his restaurants, like the Téatriz in Madrid, the Manin in Tokyo, the Felix in Hong Kong and now the Thèatron in Mexico City, one can even say that he has invented a genre.

No doubt he was inspired by the very nature of the place—the Téatriz, as its name indicates, was formerly a theater. His daring consisted in taking the place literally, so to speak, and brilliantly recycling a space that was clearly uncomfortable in and unfitted to its new function. Starck turned it into a theater of night life: from the moment they come in to their final drink, the patrons are onstage in a game that the little society of the night is so fond of, that of seeing and being seen, an alternation of voyeurism and exhibitionism. Playing with fantasies (fear of the dark and of the unknown, claustrophobia and agoraphobia, most often on a puerile note) Starck has created a kind of puppet theater in which he pulls the strings from afar.

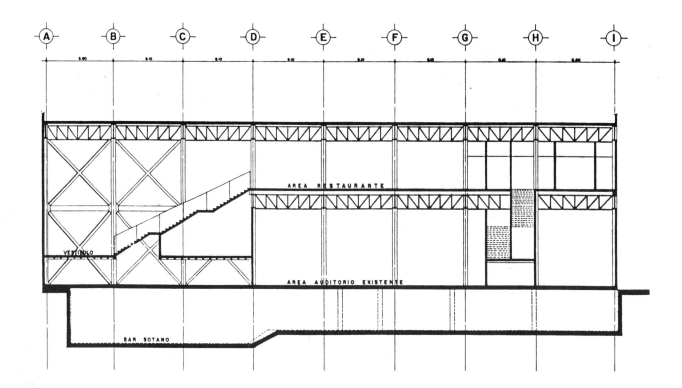

Cross-section of the
theater and floor plan of
the restaurant, showing
the disposition of the
tables.

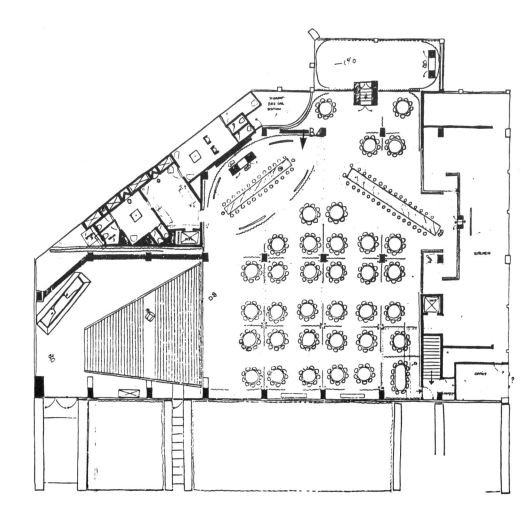

46 Thèatron, Mexico City, Mexico

The staircase rises
dramatically upward.
An ironic note,
on a landing at the
mid-point a solitary club
chair stands.

A vision of hell by Philippe Starck:
in the salon he has named Hell,
tropical wood floor in shades of red
and the cozy comfort of sofas
and assorted armchairs.

Opposite:
In the vast restaurant, diaphanous
curtains lend a touch of intimacy
without breaking up the fluidity
of the space. Subtle lighting softens
the color, and the great crystal
chandelier shines down on the long
onyx tabletop with its ornate
candelabras.

To the left of the
restaurant, a tall carved
table pays tribute to
Christopher Columbus.

Opposite:
The restrooms
are handled with
all of Starck's
customary luxury and
anti-conformity.

In Mexico City he is once again confronted with an old disaffected theater. Here again his recipe has proven itself: a gigantic entrance the entire height of the building, barely furnished with three objects and invaded by a giant blowup of a Richard Avedon photo in which Starck, with his usual finesse, has grasped the resemblance to the death masks of Mexican folklore. Facing the guests as they enter, a monumental staircase rises like a reference in reverse to Mistinguett descending her stairway to the stage. It evokes an Aztec pyramid, a platform adorned with an empty club chair flanked by a table and lamp that seems to be waiting for someone (the absent emperor or the guest himself?)

Great manipulator that he is, Starck knows how to alternate cold and warmth. After the sacred awe of mounting the staircase, the restaurant itself is pure peace and gentleness. The size of the place is brought back to the human scale with the help of chiffon draperies hanging gracefully down from high above. The lighting is warm and reassuring and its color is flattering to the complexion. The furniture is noncommittal, except for the stately table of translucent onyx surmounted by crystal chandeliers. The atmosphere of bourgeois comfort is also present in the bar, which the architect has named, perhaps a bit recklessly, Hell. Divans and ottomans, chestnut brown velvet armchairs, innocent little stools, walls of blond marquetry side by side with a chair by Gaudi. Who said that Hell is other people?

Another characteristic of these sites recuperated by Starck is the liberty with which he uses the space, without order or hierarchy, following the constraints of the place or his own imagination.

Here a bit of discotheque in violent colors, there a billiard room (!) set between a cavern wall and velvet hangings, lighted by a single bulb hanging over a colonial chair. Not the least charm of this theater according to Starck is the labyrinthian succession of different and exotic spaces that tend to abstract the visitor from reality to project him into a universe of dreams.

Disparate references in the billiard
room: a hint of glamour, a bit
of exotica and a wink at the *film noir*.
A bare bulb, heavy velvet curtains,
a chair that seems to come
from a distant jungle, black covering
on the red laquered table.

Opposite:
The ballroom, or Crazy Box, like the
corridor of a spaceship heading for
distant galaxies reflected in the
vertiginous depth of an inclined mirror.

Ismaele Marrone

La Gare

Milan, Italy

Between floor and ceiling entirely sheathed in black, the architect has placed dynamic brightly-colored structures that act as lines of force. The bright red bar, seen here in the restaurant, literally cuts across the walls to join all three spaces, restaurant, discotheque and bar/salon.

In the discotheque the sharp angles of the bar are echoed in the padded booths, disposed with their tables around the outer perimeter.

The Milan Railroad Station, popularly known as "La Centrale," is one of the architectural highlights of the city. With its heavy facade, its volumes reminiscent of a Piranesi engraving, its Mussolini-like statuary and magnificent vaulting of glass and metal, it was a striking feature of the early 1930s. When the architect Achille Stacchini gave the structure its pompous entrance and monumental stairways, it was not out of sheer caprice. The slope of the terrain made it necessary to lay the tracks on a viaduct over the existing facilities. This in turn created vast spaces on either side of the edifice, which were used for freight, while to the north the tracks pass over a series of warehouses in the form of vaulted tunnels. These tunnels gradually fell into disuse.

One common feature of night life in all our cities is that it is constantly changing. Every season, some new night spot springs up, in an effort to revive a scene perennially judged to be "getting dull." In order to make it, the new establishment has to meet two basic preconditions: it must be easily accessible (a central location) and in a place where the noise will create no problem for the environment. In Paris in the early

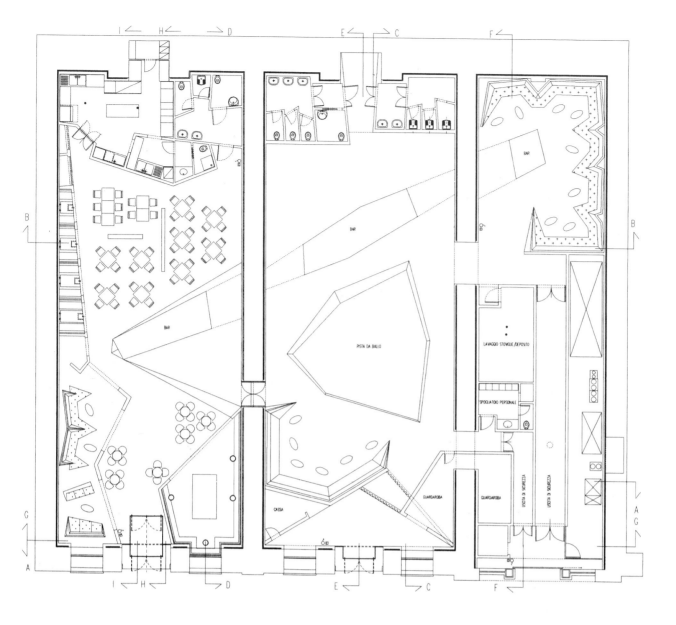

General plan showing
how the space is
virtually unified by the
diagonal of the bar.

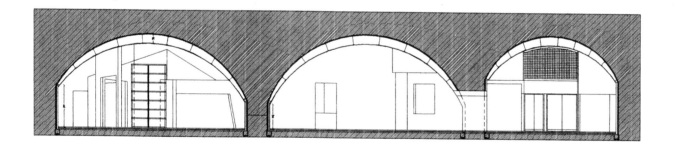

Cross-section of the
three parallel spaces.

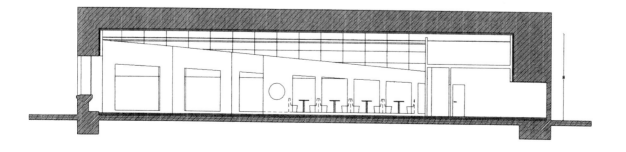

Longitudinal section
of the restaurant.

56 La Gare, Milan, Italy

postwar years, the wine-cellars of Saint-Germain-des-Prés that were turned into jazz clubs were pioneers of the genre.

There is nothing new about the combination of restaurant/bar/discotheque. It is a variation on an old theme—that of classical drama with its unities of space, time and action—updated to provide modern night owls with a single place (preferably crowded and convenient) where they can pursue, in a fairly logical sequence, their favorite pastimes of dining, drinking and dancing.

Epitomizing these attitudes, La Gare made it possible to reclaim an abandoned space near the center of town by recycling it into a multifaceted entertainment venue.

Bergamo-born architect Ismaele Marrone found himself confronted with a rather improbable space—three long brick tunnels, nearly 6 (20 feet) meters at the highest point and 11 meters (36 feet) wide. To try to scale down the huge proportions, he made a radical choice—that of covering both vaults and walls in deepest black, deeper than the black of night, and completing the ensemble with a resin floor of the same color. Against this background he placed a series of structures and prisms in vivid colors, specific objects that cut across the entire space, virtually joining together what had once been three distinct areas. The feature that springs most obviously to the eye is the bar (or bars) whose irregular shape and glaring color (bright scarlet) are repeated in the restaurant, the adjoining disco and in the inner sanctuary, the more intimate area of the bar itself.

This family of large structures with slanting shapes helps to define the space: each answers to a specific function and is color-coded—red for the bar, pink for the cloakroom, yellow for the restrooms and blue for the seating in the restaurant and disco. The only allusion to the old "Centrale" are the booths in the restaurant that remind one irresistibly of compartments on an old-fashioned train.

The volumes, by turns massive and angular, with smooth surfaces and glaring colors, seem to have their own autonomous existence. They can also be read as a sort of paradox—on one hand, toning down the scale of a place in order to make it more convivial and, on the other, an homage (barely disguised and on an utterly grandiose scale) to the era of Italian design in all its glory, to Joe Colombo, Gae Aulenti and the unfinished saga of molded plastic.

Anatomy of a colossus: on a tubular metallic structure covered with fireproof wooden panels, plasterboard and stucco laquered in bright red.

58 La Gare, Milan, Italy

In the cocktail bar,
the presence of the red
structure is felt even
more strongly because
of the smaller space.
The bar acquires almost
an animal intensity.

The one explicit allusion
to La Centrale,
the restaurant booths
that look like train
compartments.

Opposite:
Colors strike with
whiplash force, elements
seem liberated from
their inertia, life surges
out of the pure
movement of simple
forms and seizes
the entire space.

In the general ambiance of destabilization, where our most ordinary landmarks lose their meaning, the restrooms are not left out. Circles of light embedded in the floor, sharp angles and glaring yellow walls.

Around the dance
floor, touches of blue
exalt the triumph
of red, under a "sky"
of deepest black.

Alfredo Arribas, Miguel Morte and Javier Mariscal

Torres de Avila

Barcelona, Spain

An imitation fortress that Walt Disney could call his own, reconverted for the people of the night to worship the mythical rendezvous of Sun and Moon.

Opposite:
A terrace with a ghostly glow that competes with the city lights in the distance and the walkway between between the towers of Sun and Moon. The skylight bears a host of signs and symbols— cabalistic, astrological, planetary and esoteric— all transmuted in a spirit of pure fantasy. In the foregound, several skeletal-looking chairs.

Ever since their inception in the middle of the 19th century, Universal Expositions have served as a pretext to present to the world the state of science and technology at a given time, a kind of cross-section through the history of progress. Traditionally, the host country has added a more popular feature that shows off, often in a spirit of popular folklore and with more than a little nostalgia, the cultural heritage of its provinces or regions. In Barcelona in 1929, Spain had also bowed to this golden rule. On the flank of the mountain of Montjuich the builders placed a *muy típico* Spanish village, earthy and picturesque, and aptly named it El Pueblo Español. For added dignity and solemnity, they gave it a monumental gate as an entranceway, a replica of some unlikely fortress defended by the ghost of El Cid Campeador.

Floor plan of the ground level and vertical section of the whole structure.

Section of the Moon Tower with its oval cupola, and the Sun Tower, with an elevator leading to the terrace.

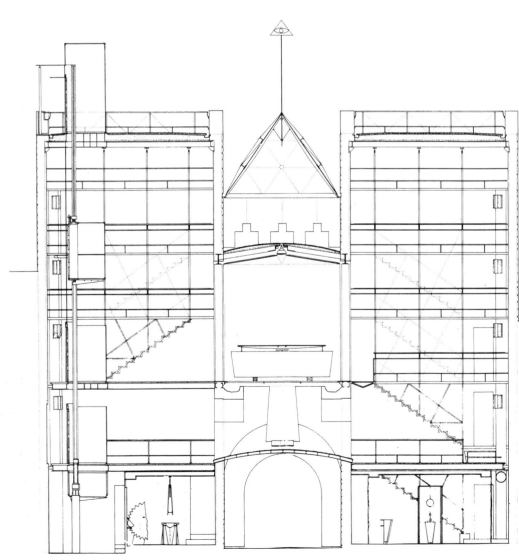

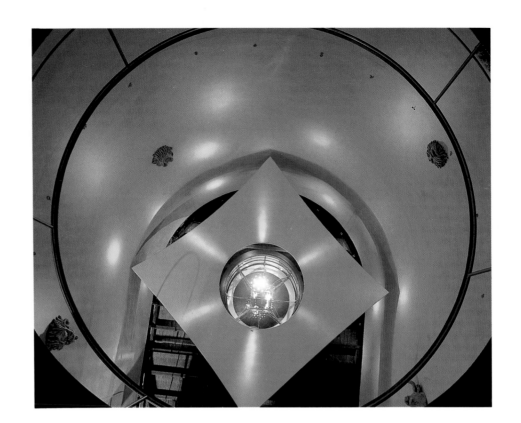

Looking upward to the
device of the artificial
sun with its mobile
oculus that modulates
the rays.

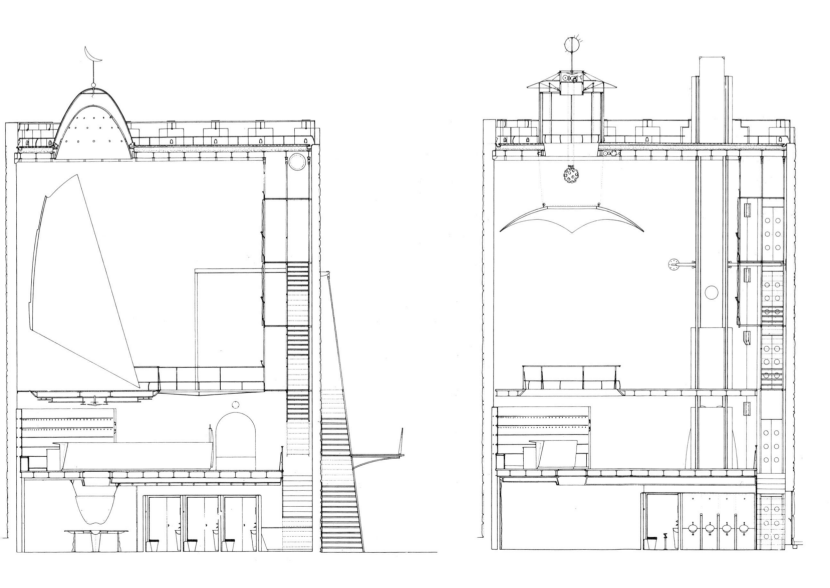

Entrance between the two towers. With dim lighting under the low archway or recessed into the walls, the atmosphere here is still that of an old castle.

As Spain was preparing for the 1992 Olympics, the aim was to give Montjuich back its luster, to recall the splendor of times gone by. On the site of the Pueblo they erected a replica of the German Pavilion of 1929, designed by Mies van der Rohe and an heroic symbol of modern architecture. But the few remaining traces of the Pueblo posed a problem. What in the world could they do with the massive and rather graceless structure that stood so tall and bold right at the western edge of the Olympic site? It didn't take long to come up with an answer. As Barcelona had now recovered its once-famed swinging night life, they would turn the spot into a meeting place for the new nightclubbers. Chosen to design the interior were the stars of Catalan design: Alfredo Arribas, Miguel Forte and Javier Mariscal.

Short of resorting to dynamite, there was no way to modify the outer appearance of the gate, like some Disneyesque version of the medieval towers of Avila. The architects did nothing more on the outside than to hang an attractive colored banner on the front of the facade. But the work they carried out inside was a brilliant exercise, an artistic *tour de force*. After passing through the vault, the visitor enters the building by a staircase detached from and parallel to the inner facade and by a suspended gangway, clearly of shipboard inspiration. Behind this facade and taking up the whole width of the structure, the architects grouped together all the vertical circulations, thus liberating three high volumes, the two lateral ones contained in the towers themselves and dedicated respectively to the moon and the sun and the rectangular space between them (representing... who knows? dawn perhaps, or dusk...)

The three volumes have a similar configuration: a vast bar on the lower level, a smaller, more intime one suspended over the first, and the whole thing topped off by a terrace, as with a sort of hat. Having resolved the problems posed by the site, the architects gave free rein to their fantasy. Repeated references, luminous and brightly colored, to the themes of sun and moon are found everywhere—on the walls, the furnishings and decorative objects. Not a space is without them—here a constellation, there a milky way or an astrological sign, a phantasmagoric accumulation of cabalistic signs, enough to make one's head spin. The crowning jewel of the work is the terrace with its three skylights of different shape and color, and its chairs with their bone-like bases and pale-colored, oddly-shaped backs, looking like some sort of extra-terrestrial insects, where the night owls can wait for the "rosy-fingered dawn" to reach the sky of Barcelona...

The wire mesh door and shiplike ropes under the banner showing a mysterious knight and a green serpent.

From the courtyard, the building is approached like a vessel at sea: a little staircase detached from the facade leads to a suspended footbridge.

Between the towers, a little bar in colors of the dawn snuggles under a pyramid-like structure with star-shaped facets whose summit goes through to the terrace. The eye of Horus gazes down on the scene.

A more spacious bar on the lower level stands on glass flooring that cunningly multiplies views and reflections. The line of bottles seems to be borne on shining pommels of a row of swords. At the rear of the room, a metal walkway leads to other bars on the same level.

On a red orange background, incized drawings reveal the concrete underneath. Under the masonic sign in the center, all the symbolism of Torres de Avila is contained in this wall.

Opalescent light, a ring
of tiny signs in relief,
a lion's head and
a Medusa—one
of the high platforms
of the Moon Tower.
The central opening
looks down on the
luminous ramps of the
large bar.

On the lunar level, the
apogee of theatrical
mise-en-scene. An oval
half-cupola envelopes
a little bar suspended
in the milky way.
The underside of the
platform looks like a
flying saucer, marked
with the 12 signs of
the zodiac, that seems
to be landing or taking
off over the large bar.

Aldo Rossi and Ettore Sottsass Jr., Kuramata Shiro, Gaetano Pesce, Alfredo Arribas

Palazzo hotel: bars and night club

Fukuoka, Japan

In Il Palazzo, the hotel
designed by Aldo
Rossi, the theme
of the bar has been
conjugated in a mode
resembling those old
films where each
director contributed
one sketch.
Each bar has been
given to a designer
of international renown.
Here, in the Liston
by Gaetano Pesce,
an explosion of red
with contrasts of black
and yellow, where
fragmented spaces
separated by false
screens cascade down
a staircase splashed
with color.

The port of Fukuoka is situated in the south of the Japanese archipelago, facing the Korean straits. Far from the vast conurbations of Tokyo and Osaka, it is distinguished by the relatively orderly quality of its urban structure compared to the chaos commonly associated with Japanese cities.

Fukuoka was not particularly well-known until the end of the 1980s, when two large-scale projects attracted media attention to the city. The first was a planning scheme announced by the famous architect Isozaki Arata, which was to call upon the greatest names of international architecture. Steven Holl, Rem Koolhaas, Christian de Portzamparc and Oscar Tusquets all came to build housing for the city. The second was the construction of the Hotel Palazzo, given to the late great Italian architect Aldo Rossi, with Ushida Shigaru in charge of the interior design. To make it even more interesting, the client suggested that Rossi surround himself with a selection of the best designers of the day to create the hotel's bars and night club. An all-star cast was recruited, including the Italians Ettore Sottsass Jr., Gaetano Pesce and Rossi himself, the late Japanese Kuramata Shiro and the Catalan Alfredo Arribas. Aside from considerations of attracting public attention, they wanted to create spaces that would be strongly differentiated, yet consistent with the general design of the building, by vocation an international hotel. The bars occupy small lateral buildings on either side of the hotel. The night club is installed in the basement of the building itself.

The bar called the El Dorado was conceived by Rossi and displays all his usual obsessions—an archetypal space with a double pitched roof supported by an exposed metal brace; over the bar a gable pierced with an oculus and a grid-patterned facade lit with a golden light (whence the name El Dorado) against a background of reddish travertine; a floor of polished gray granite, simple furniture in bright red and pale gray, matching the color of the walls, and a staircase of stainless steel with risers made of glass blocks. Even on a small scale, Rossi thinks architecturally. On the wall hangs a large drawing, one of those colorful urban landscapes of which he had the secret.

In the bar designed by Sottsass, which has the odd name of Zibibbo, the architect's intentions are clearly both ostentatious and ironic. The steeply pitched ceilings are covered with golden

Under giant stalactite formations in softly
voluptuous shapes with speckled surfaces,
the bar undulates on a floor with an irregular
geometric pattern, glittering and pointilistic.

From higher up, a double sky constellated
with minuscule suspended lights that cover
the acute angle of the roof and lure the spectator
to the venimous charms of some mythical Hollywood
version of Shanghai.

74 Palazzo hotel, Fukuoka, Japan

Who can resist a log cabin under the stars?
Ettore Sottsass Jr. plays the card of an object
within an object. His two-level bar, the Zibbibo,
is an ironic architectural statement: a gray marble
colonnade supports a mezzanine with a black wall
and a cutout window opening.

constellations on a deep blue background, while heavy marble pillars support a black-walled mezzanine with a window. Here Sottsass has played with the idea of an object within an object by marking the space with two constructions of bright yellow wood that fragment it and divide it into smaller more intimate units.

The Liston Bar is the work of Gaetano Pesce. The layout in tiers flanked by a lateral staircase gives Pesce a chance to develop fragmented spaces in a random and violent esthetic. The convoluted shapes, furniture with organic accents, a strident color scheme, dominated by red, yellow and black—all features he has accustomed us to—take on here a more ambiguous dimension, certainly more Chinese in inspiration then Japanese, closer to our idea of an opium den or Asian bordello than to the typical Japanese teahouse.

Kuramata's Oslomova Bar is just the opposite of the Liston. A bright, clear room with delicate colors, lightly delineated by glass and color-edged *plexiglass*, a series of red and blue verticals set off against an apricot ground and discreetly punctuated by lighting, make this space immaterial almost to the point of disappearance. A final sublime note—the little flowers suspended in their transparent cylinders, the architect's trademark.

With Arribas we enter another world—a cross-cultural, ever-shifting world of cosmopolitan night life, where anything can happen. Spread over two levels in the basement of the hotel, with its own separate entrance, this vast space is called Barna Crossing. From the lava staircase with its little portholes to the glass cage of the discotheque, from the hanging restaurant to the various bars (one of which has been dubbed the Vitamin Bar) the spaces succeed one another in a jumble of jagged shapes and glaring or iridescent colors. Strobe lights and torrents of decibels, this is the universe of today's young jet set... or is it a scene from one of the levels of hell?

78 Palazzo hotel, Fukuoka, Japan

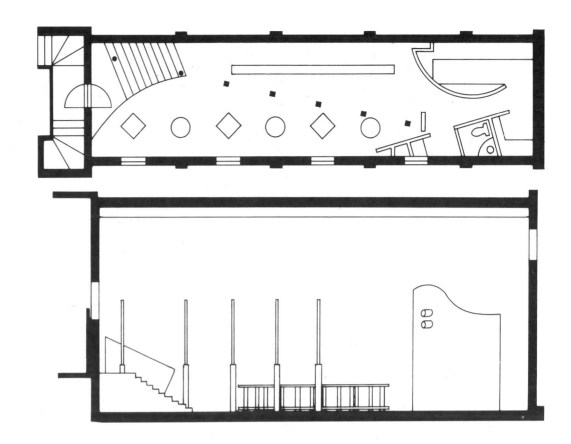

Obslomova, a dream of immateriality. The bar according to Shiro Kuramata: a space of light and transparency, belonging to the realm of air more than to that of night. In tones of peach or apricot, shiny walls and ceilings reflect the delicate light diffused by the tall slim light fixtures. Their fine vertical lines rise to become nearly invisible, with rosebuds encased in glass floating as if in weightlessness.

Aldo Rossi and Ettore Sottsass Jr., Kuramata Shiro, Gaetano Pesce, Alfredo Arribas 79

In the El Dorado, designed by Rossi himself, he repeats the themes used throughout the hotel. Above the bar the gridlike pattern of the hotel's main facade, magnified by a golden light. Another reference, the marbled red travertine also used on the hotel's facade. Rossi makes the space his own through use of strong signs, like his obsessive variations on the triangle— in a major key, in the gable pierced with a large oculus and the exposed metal brace; in a minor key—on the steel doors punctuated with a little eye of light and in the little pyramids that crown the stainless steel stairposts.

Aldo Rossi and Ettore Sottsass Jr., Kuramata Shiro, Gaetano Pesce, Alfredo Arribas 81

82 Palazzo hotel, Fukuoka, Japan

Descent to the inner sanctum: halfway
between an ancestral cave dwelling
and a spaceship revisited by Hollywood.

Opposite:
Only the sound barrier separates bar and dance
floor. The light show so dear to pop concerts
floods the smooth metal walls of the bar
with all the colors of the spectrum. Another
cinematic touch, that staircase that might
have been discarded by a spaceship.

Vicenzo Iavicoli and Maria Luisa Rossi

Kabuto

Tokyo, Japan

Armchairs with neo-baroque lines undulate in this Italo-Japanese *pas-de-deux*.

An appealing hybrid of Latin culture, contemporary design and Japanese culinary traditions, the Kabuto takes its name from the intriguing metal helmets that crown the tables.

The Kirin brewery, maker of the famous Japanese beer, long ago learned the media value of architecture. The firm was among the first to attempt to enhance its brand image by calling upon an architect both famous and out-of-the-ordinary.

The gleaming metal machine built for the firm by Takamatsu Shin made its mark and has remained engraved in memory.

With this restaurant Kirin is testing a new concept of marketing. A traditional Japanese dish called Shabu-Shabu is a mixture of meat, vegetables and tofu that the diner cooks at the table in a pot of boiling broth. Kirin has come up with a variant in which the meat is replaced by fish. Called Kaisen-Shabu, it will be featured in a chain of restaurants of the same name, which will also serve to give Kirin beer a discreet though widespread publicity.

The architectural firm commissioned to carry out the interior design is that of Iavicoli & Rossi, two of those nomads of international design that one finds in all the great capitals of the world. Here they have chosen to intermingle the signs of two cultures, Japanese and Italian, and to take their inspiration from the theme of fish, which is, after all, the basis of the recipe...

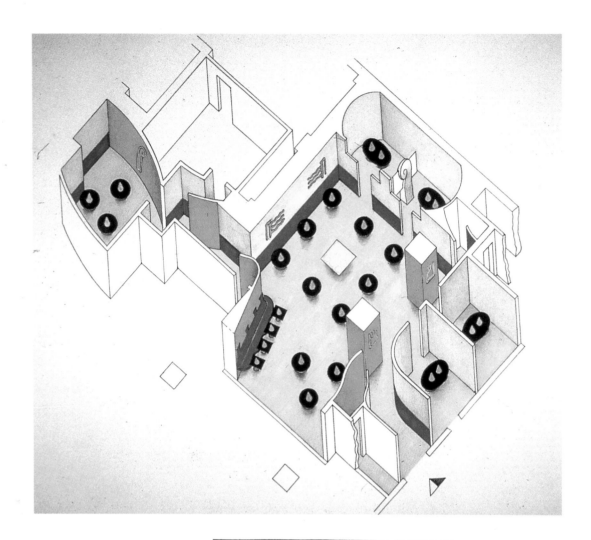

Plan and axonometric
projection of the
restaurant, showing
the layout of the private
dining areas around
the main restaurant
room.

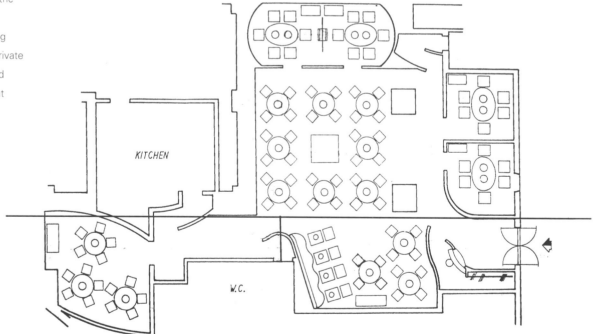

KITCHEN

W.C.

The restaurant space corresponds to local customs in terms of dining out. The architects have simply created, along with the main dining room, two small private salons and another area that can be divided by a removable screen in order to offer large open spaces and more intimate ones. The entrance is through a vestibule whose curved walls soften the volume and shield the dining room proper from view of the entering customers. The truly Italian touch is the manner in which the walls and partitions have been treated—with a range of colors that evoke the distant Mediterranean. Cobalt blue contrasts with sandy beige and ocher to form the background of a peaceful decor, highlighted here and there by rippling patterns that resemble golden waves.

The furnishings designed by the architects could belong to either culture: blond wood chairs with sinuous lines, covered with colored suede, are of a neo-baroque genre that is all the rage in Milan as well as in Tokyo. The tables, with their built-in cooking apparatus, have black tops on a two-colored base of black and gold made of two truncated cones joined together at their narrow ends. Each table has a built-in cooking pot to hold the simmering Kaisen-Shabu broth. Since the pot needed to have a cover designed for it, Iavicoli and Rossi came up with a strange-looking object that adds an unusual touch to the whole place. A cone of gilded metal decorated with small indented designs and with two lateral wings, it resembles the helmet of a samurai or a medieval knight. Or is it the pointed hat of some Japanese sorcerer? These curious little pot covers and the movable screen topped with its sweeping volute constitute the high points in the off-beat attraction of the place.

Sketch of the furniture for the private dining rooms.

A provocatively eerie note is added by the helmet that covers a cooking device built into the table. The black tabletop rests on a base of black and gold formed by two truncated cones placed end to end.

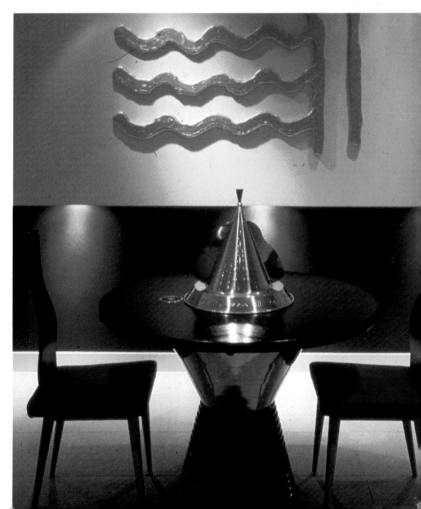

88 Kabuto, Tokyo, Japan

A canape of blue waves faces blond wood armchairs
covered in chocolate brown suede.

Opposite:
Across the oceans, an homage to the Mediterranean.
Golden waves in relief on the walls above a broad band
of cobalt blue set off by tones of sand and ocher.
The maritime reference is not gratuitous—under the winged
helmets simmers a fish specialty. In a central position,
the large square table on its upside down pyramid takes
on an appearance of ceremonial altar.

Detail of the volute on
the mobile separation
screen placed between
the private dining
rooms. This element is
sufficiently emblematic
to be found repeated
in the door handles
of the entrance.

90 Kabuto, Tokyo, Japan

The rounded volumes of the vestibule give a glimpse of the inside without revealing it completely. In the wall that hides the cloakroom an opening repeats the shape (though smaller and in the opposite direction) of a sideways heart used in the entrance canopy.

Takasaki Masaharu

Restaurant

Asu-Kuju, Japan

An architecture that set itself a challenging task to restore the links between man and the spiritual world. The building, posed by architect Takasaki Masaharu between Mount Asu and Mount Kuju, makes no attempt to hide. With its extremely free forms and its senses deployed, it is conceived as a sort of observation post or privileged perception point for the surrounding nature.

The main entrance: an effect of rising perspective multiplied overhead by the underside of the steps of the staircase of the floor above. The beige ocher color varies with the shifting quality of the light.

The Westerner, brought up in the cult of reason, is always slightly bewildered by Japanese culture, with its multitude of little gods that inhabit all the artifacts of everyday life. In the same way, he is perplexed by the way the Japanese tend to see architecture as a mediation between man and the universe. In short, where the West is pragmatic, Japan is spiritual.

Thus, when the architect Takasaki Masaharu was commissioned to build a restaurant in a natural park, he summed up what his client wanted as "a playful cosmology." It was to be situated in an unspoiled site, a valley between Mount Asu and Mount Kuju, at an altitude of 1,100 meters (3,600 feet). The architect was well aware of the fact that the building would be the only manmade element in the entire landscape. But this did not lead him to try to dissimulate or underplay it. The edifice is clearly visible for miles around and its elongated shape and curving roof and prominent surfaces asserts its calm presence against the backdrop of the mountains. The one natural touch is its color, a soft ocher/beige.

The curved roof, fluid volumes, and horizontal position integrate the building into the mountainous landscape without clash or conflict.

Jubilant play of concrete around the central void shaped like an elongated ring. The many clusters of columns and the great staircase in the form of an amphitheater give the ensemble a strong skyward thrust.

94 Restaurant, Asu-Kuju, Japan

The two restaurants situated
at either end of the first floor
ellipse are linked by a peripheral
promenade bordered
on the side opposite
the staircase by metal railings
that resemble a giant spiderweb.

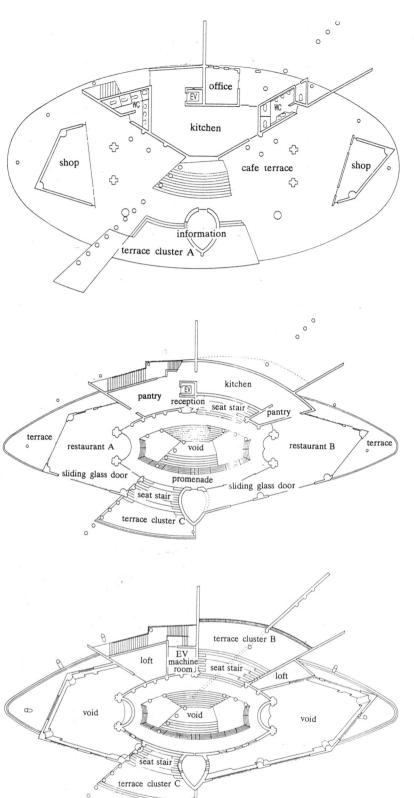

A parking area, a two-branched driveway, one for deliveries (even in Japan, food doesn't fall from the sky), the other for visitors, constitute the access to the building. A large passageway, its roof formed by the underside of the tiers above, leads to a courtyard. From there a broad staircase shaped like an amphitheater takes you to the two upper levels. On a plan of a narrowed ellipse the complex has a ring-like layout, the practical spaces being set out between a central void and a peripheral promenade, a way perhaps of indicating that these spaces occupy a shifting location between the centripetal forces of group and society and the centrifugal ones of nature and the cosmos. Functionally, the complex is intended as a stopping point for tourists. It comprises three levels: the first holds an information office, two shops, a kitchen and an open-air café terrace. The second has two restaurants, extended by terraces, at the northwest and southeast of the building on either side of a vast kitchen and separated from the central void by a promenade and the kitchen. On the third level are the workshops and technical facilities as well as two upper terraces accessible to visitors.

On this rational overall scheme, the architect has designed a free-form building. Its concrete structure is exposed everywhere—heavy slanting posts on the outside and columns around the central void support the floors and the flights of broad steps that invite passers-by to use them as seats. Another cluster of columns bear vertical walls that reach upward toward the sky and yet another, in the amphitheater, is a play of pure form whose symbolic intentions seem indecipherable.

As the architect says, the experience of nature cannot be limited to looking at a landscape through a large window. Into the curving volumes of his building he has inserted openings of all shapes and sizes—small triangles, long narrow slits and elongated oculi serve as counterpoint for the large slanted windows of the restaurants, a manner of framing chosen bits of landscape, here a horizon, there a constellation, elsewhere a nearby mountaintop. The furniture is of a spartan simplicity and the color scheme of blue and violet punctuated by large yellow circles adds to the calculated extravagance of the building. "Architecture," says Takasaki Masaharu, "must restore our relations with matters of the spirit."

Plans of the three levels and cross-section.

Opposite:
The night brings
a spectacular mutation:
a spaceship sending out
eerie beams of white
light.

96 Restaurant, Asu-Kuju, Japan

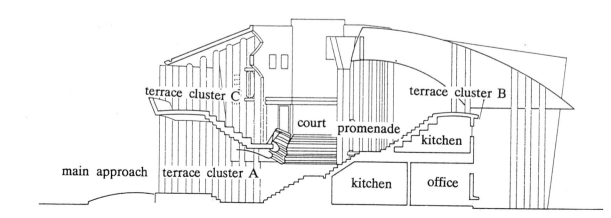

Large windows slanted inward
offer a sumptuous panorama
around the rooms of the
restaurant, extended by
terraces. In counterpoint,
long narrow openings, triangles
and oculi focus on selected bits
of sky or countryside.

The minimal furniture does
nothing to distract the eye
from the landscape, while
the astonishing violet color
highlighted with large orange
circles dramatizes the
impressive volume of the room.

Wolfgang Kaitna, Rüdiger Reichel and Kurt Smetana with Oskar Putz

Kix Bar

Vienna, Austria

An axonometric projection as a support for the chromatic study.

Decor as abstraction, geometry and polychromatic study. In a 19th-century Viennese building three architects and a painter give us a virtuoso rendition of the "fusion-of-the-arts" fantasy so beloved by the avant-garde movements of the 1920s.

Multiplying orthogonal cutouts creates a depth of field where the eye plunges into the subtle shifts of color.

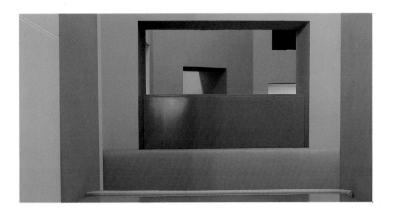

The Kix Bar draws its inspiration less from the traditional Viennese coffee house than from the experimentations of the DeStijl movement active in the Netherlands in the 1920s. In two examples of that era, the De Unie café in Rotterdam, designed by J.P.P. Oud, and the Aubette in Strasbourg (a collaboration between Van Doesburg and the Arps), the dominant element of the architecture was the use of color applied to a geometric structure. The physical trace of both these realizations has more or less disappeared although their memory lives on. The facade of the De Unie was recently restored—the reconstruction is undoubtedly faithful, but marred by a contemporary interior design of no great quality. As for the Aubette, all that remain are several old black and white photos. From what we know of Van Doesburg and his attachment to the principles set out

Indirect and neutral
lighting, a floor covering
with a simple diamond
pattern in light gray
metal, furniture of pure
geometric lines, all the
elements deliberately
self-effacing to exalt
the pure perception of
colors.

General plan.

Opposite:
Inside the facade,
near the entrance,
two vertical windows
opening onto
Bäckerstrasse rise
the entire height of
the room.

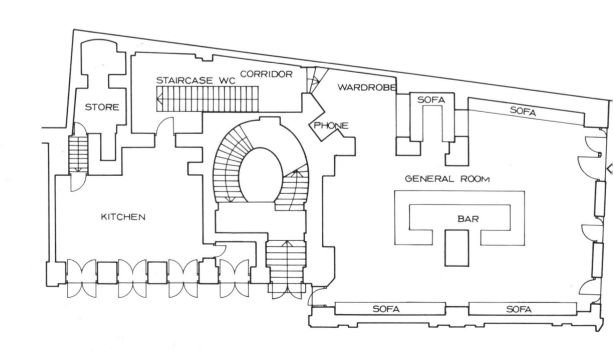

by Mondrian, we can only presume that color was of primary importance.

The Kix Bar is an attempt to reinvent a genre. In all the age-old dreams of "fusion of the arts," a partnership between architects and painters is one of the great fantasies. Experience has often shown it to be a perilous one, for it demands not only that both parties should see eye to eye, but that they should respect each other's work, agree on the boundaries between their domains and be totally devoted to the common project. It is a synergy of just this kind that seems to have operated between the architects and the plastic artist of the Kix Bar.

The aim of the architects was to lighten and pare down the existing space so as to occupy the maximum volume. What remains is the supporting structure of this traditional 19th-century Viennese building, with its too-high ceilings and wall recesses. The architects proceeded to install the kitchen and storage space at the rear of the premises, then placed the bar in a central position (working around the massive sustaining pillar) and laid down an industrial floor-covering with a pattern of small lozenges. Now the coast was clear for the painter to do his part, i.e., to recompose and reorder the entire space. Oskar Putz worked methodically—applying color in large rectilinear swathes and following a sophisticated palette in which the primary colors are definitely in the minority.

Goethe was perhaps the first to point out that the addition of colors tends to darken a space. At the Kix the shades of blue, intense green, slightly muted red and luminous orange applied in broad vertical bands seem to bring the walls closer, giving the place a greater intimacy. Here and there, usually just above seat level, a horizontal band is used in order to moderate the altogether immoderate height of the room. Here Putz most certainly kept in mind Albers's warnings about the juxtaposition of dominant colors vertically (easy) and horizontally (more difficult).

The artist also plays with contrasting quantities (a notion once brought out by Johannes Itten), which enables him to emphasize some of the colored areas and to attenuate others. Aside from the immediate impression of strong sensuality, the virtuosity of the use of color is manifest. With this manipulation of its geometry through the use of color and the playing around with depth of field, the Kix Bar has become a space that is studied and playful at the same time.

The clear predominance of verticals is tempered by several horizontal bands just above the level of the seats.

In the original volume, full of protrusions and recesses, each section of wall, including the cloakroom, serves as a support for the color.

Opposite:
The rectanglular bar, designed to encompass the massive supporting pillar, occupies the center of the space. An inner band of light, the only source of direct white light, calls attention to the contours, underlined by wood and metal rails.

Daniel Freixes and Vicente Miranda

Cocteleria Zsa-Zsa

Barcelona, Spain

A brilliant demonstration of how to turn a major defect into an irresistable asset. The entrance to the Zsa Zsa is through two long corridors adorned with traditional carpets that have been artistically cut up and reassembled into a patchwork by graphic artist Peret. The lighting, programmed to change constantly in direction and intensity, modifies the appearance of the of the glazed surfaces, which become by turns mirrors, reflectors or transparent windows.

Once upon a time, before the Spanish Civil War, Barcelona was one of the hot spots of European night life, where artists and writers of varied styles and many nationalities haunted the cafés and bordellos of the Ramblas. In the tragic aftermath of the war, the city went into a long eclipse before coming back to life in the early 1980s. In those first heady years, when a youthful population was celebrating its liberation, a series of new bars and discos came into being, one of which was a cocktail bar called the Zsa-Zsa. Was it the quality of its tapas? Or the luminous severity of its design? Or perhaps its street sign depicting a legendary blonde actress, all pink and buxom? It may have been a cocktail of all these ingredients. Whatever the case, the Zsa-Zsa has lived on to become a reference.

From the outset, its premises presented two very severe constraints. First, and not the least difficult, was the fact that it was located on the ground floor with its front cut right down the middle by the building entrance, leaving two awkward corridors, long narrow spaces, on either side. Second, because of its location, it had to be absolutely soundproof, no simple requirement for an establishment that is noisy by its very nature. The architects Freixes and Miranda affronted these difficulties head on, and turned them to their advantage. They built a box within a box, making use of false ceilings, a floating floor, walls set away from the building sides and carefully insulated against sound. As for the two parallel corridors that form the entrance to the Zsa-Zsa, they turned them into a sort of shifting, shining sideshow. The two outer walls of the perimeter are like two long glass boxes with an ever-changing light program, sometimes translucent, sometimes reflecting. The walls that separate the bar from the

building entrance were covered with cloth to absorb the sound, a multicolored fabric in a geometric patchwork pattern designed by the graphic artist Peret. The reflection of the patchwork in the glass boxes with the moving lights creates a glittering kaleidoscope of color that imbues the entire space.

For such an apparatus to function, the surroundings had to be free of opaque structures or cumbersome objects. The architects installed a series of little tables held up by slender columns of stainless metal along with metallic stools on fine thin legs. The light fixtures also are nothing more than small round reflectors. All these self-effacing elements are barely seen amid the surrounding luminosity and the entire central space is left empty. The bar is placed diagonally near the rear of the room and the control booth where the sound and light are programmed is behind it. Together, they occupy a minimum of visual space. Faced with a daunting problem of design, Freixes and Miranda have come up with an efficient solution, and they have done it without resorting to any excessive or trendy effect of the moment (as is sometimes the case with modern Catalan design). Perhaps this is the true reason for the longevity of the Cocteleria Zsa-Zsa.

Efficient in function, consistent in appearance: at the tops of the columns, stainless steel trays like those used in the bar serve as reflectors over a fine halogen bulb...

Floor plan and lateral cross-sections.

Opposite:
In the second corridor, fine birch panels placed behind the glass walls create a mirror effect, multiplying the kaleidoscope of the patchwork carpet.

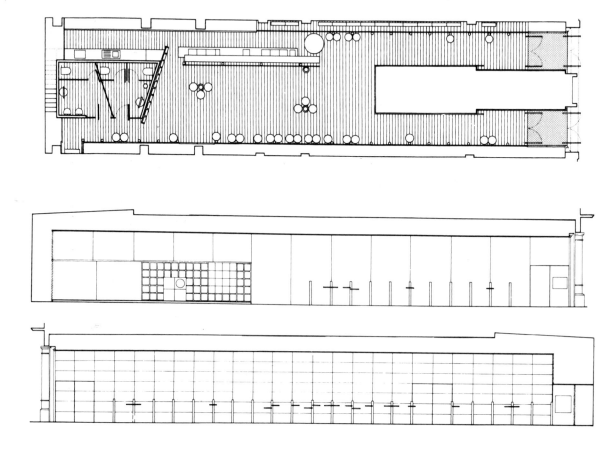

The bar, bathed in golden light, is built around a luminous screen that creates a fade-out effect on all the surrounding colors.

Stainless steel columns and colonnettes holding trays are all that is needed to provide table space. Add some slender metal bar stools and—presto!— a great amount of space is liberated.

Facing the bar, an entire wall
of luminous glass rectangles.
At the rear, a coffered wooden
unit holds a well-insulated
control booth that programs
sound and light.

The shiny steel effaces
all sharp contours,
reflecting darts of light
and ever-shifting forms.
In this space, relations
between objects take
precedence over the
objects themselves.

Detail of trays attached
to small free-standing
columns.

Irmfried Windbichler

Nachtexpress
Graz, Austria

With contrasting or
even clashing colors,
elegant materials side
by side with those of
industrial inspiration,
a paradoxical harmony
grows out of a masterly
use of dissonance.
The music bar occupies
two underground
levels, around flights
of staircases covered
with marble slabs.
Natural light penetrates
diagonally to the
bottom, reflected from
a glass balcony on the
upper level.

With his strong predilection for small spaces where he can develop in a dense and concentrated manner all the facets of his talent, the Austrian architect Irmfried Windbichler must have been delighted to be given this music bar in the very heart of Graz.

A graduate of the Technical University of Graz, Windbichler has, since 1985, carried out many works in which he has affirmed his ability to think of space as a dynamic of exchange and communication. Notable among his many realizations was an experimental project built at Hartmannsdorf and consisting of building socially-subsidized housing based on one-family units. He also did some work in the design of street accessories, notably, creating prototypes for the bus shelters of the town of Graz.

The volume of this bar, a cube divided into two levels, posed a problem of visual, as well as physical, communication. In addition, the careful attention paid to the treatment of natural light (given that these premises are in a basement) is most unusual and worthy of particular note. Marked contrasts in form, color and material also help to define this space as one particularly well-suited to the cultural and recreational habits of contemporary society.

The first level was approximately rectangular but the second, more irregular in shape, resembled one of those residual spaces that are always more difficult to deal with. To create a link between these two zones, Windbichler had the idea of using the staircase both as opening and separation, i.e., linking the two levels while at the same time emphasizing the split-level feeling.

On the upper level there is a bar, the disc jockey's booth and two small balconies from which one can see what is happening below. The lower level, larger in size, combines two distinct spaces—one devoted to musical activities, with a small stage and seats for the audience and another, on the opposite side, with a bar and small tables where one can eat or drink standing up.

With this division, the architect's intention clearly appears. He wanted to have two different atmospheres coexist, one on each floor, so as to give each floor its originality. The ground floor is therefore mainly based on direct exchange, with an active ambience that favors meeting and exchange. Downstairs the approach is more classic, with zones of privacy, further encouraged by the possibility of listening to live music.

The entrance, at street level, communicates with both areas by means of a staircase. Clients can remain upstairs, to drink and talk, or they can go directly downstairs where they

The first-floor bar, an intermingling of jazzy lines in a dynamic space that focuses on encounters and conversation. The metal bar, with a series of indentations, is highlighted in a halo of red and flanked on the right by the DJ's cabin.

Floor plans: left, the lower level devoted to live music; right, the street level bar.

Opposite:
A deconstructed effect for a small space cleverly constructed all in verticality. The two ambiences communicate visually by the transparent staircase and the glass balconies with their sharp lines.

Facing one of the bars in the concert space, a small stage for the musicians.

Following pages:
From the staircase a double perspective that takes in the two levels. Below, a row of seats resembling those of a train give the bar the connotation recalled in its name, Nachtexpress.

Downward view on a fragment of decor showing the impeccable design.

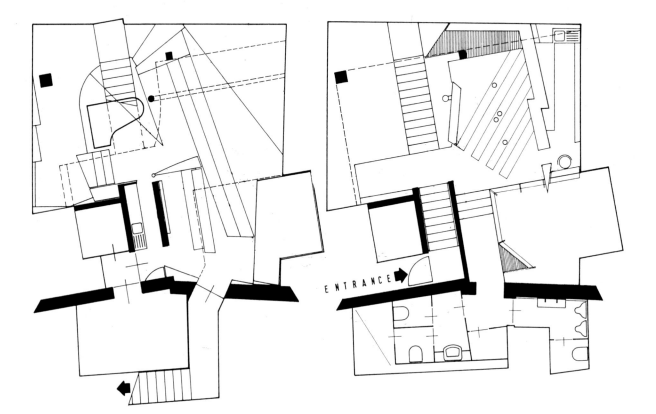

ENTRANCE

will find a more muted, less agitated ambience. From this entrance a downward view encompasses both areas, accentuating still more the feeling of proximity and conviviality. The ensemble has a harmony, born, paradoxically, out of a confrontation of cold materials like steel and glass with other elegant materials of high quality.

An opening in the upper part allows the natural light to hit the staircase wall, creating in the lower part a luminosity that is most original and remarkably effective.

By meeting his challenge, that of creating unity and free circulation between the two floors of the Nachtexpress, Windbichler offers a fine example of the renewal of Austrian design in recent years.

Borek Sipek
Beddington's
Amsterdam, Netherlands

A change of image accomplished by altering a few elements without touching the structure, floor plan or the furniture. Borek Sipek's first strategic point of intervention was the entrance, where he placed the curving sinuous structures that envelope it in a yellow-orange warmth and add a humorous note of theatricality.

Plan of the restaurant.

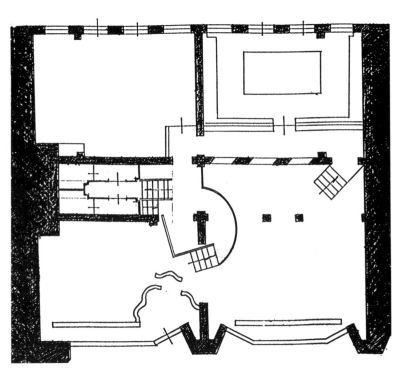

With its geography of bridges and canals, Amsterdam has often been likened to Venice, but if their common element is water, the one that clearly differentiates them in the traveler's mind is the light. As in the paintings of Vermeer and Spilliaert, the pale glow of arching northern skies recalls long ago images of flat landscapes where little scudding clouds cast ever-moving reflections on the dikes and polders.

This light in movement permeates Beddington's, giving it warmth and radiance. The original restaurant, owned by Jeanny Beddington, had been designed by the architect Koen van Velsen in 1986. When it became clear that the place no longer corresponded to the aspirations of its users, the Czech architect and designer Borek Sipek was called upon to remodel the restaurant's strategic points: the facade, the entrance and the restrooms. With limited time and funds, Sipek had to succeed in redefining a style. Completed in June 1989, the transformations met the wishes of the owner: to modify the interior and exterior appearance of the place without recourse to any reconstruction work.

The main problem Sipek had to solve was that the facade, almost entirely of plate glass, deprived diners of all sense of privacy, particularly as the restaurant was so small that its entire area felt exposed to the street. Sipek quickly saw that to restore the feeling of privacy there would have to be a screen between outside and inside. At the same time, however, the screen should not be allowed to destroy the wonderful natural light, a great asset of the place. This double constraint, to isolate but not to darken, was the challenge for the architect, and the resulting design has amply met the specifications. Two protective screens were put up, forming a physical and visual limit with the outside. But the screens contain rectangular openings of different sizes, which break up the light as it flows through them and pours into the room, constructing a geometry of brightness and creating an auspicious atmosphere for conviviality and confidential conversation. With their geometric openwork, these screens may evoke (depending on the mood of the sky and the eye of the beholder) the pigeon lofts of painted brick one sees in nearby Flanders or the *moucharabia* of faraway harems in more exotic climes. Aside from their function of protective filter, they also make the setting conducive to dreaming and meditation.

A further vector of intimacy, the yellow and ocher tones of the two screens contrast with the cold architecture of the building's glazed facade. This same color scheme, with its soft, mellow tones, is also used in the design of the entrance.

In his choice of three sinuous structures, Sipek opted for a theatrical effect. The intense color and curving lines have the voluptuousness of a theater curtain, while at the same time they recall the waves of the sea that is never far away. Lastly, the little rounded entrance space evokes the revolving doors of the old hotels of days gone by, with the one difference, of course, that they are not transparent. Unlike those doors, which gave the patron an immediate glimpse inside, these curved surfaces fully screen the interior and seem to hint, with humor, of a surprise that waits inside for those who enter.

The last zone where Sipek was asked to intervene was the restrooms. Here, by completely redesigning the accessories and using a decoration based on ceramics, he has managed to create a whole new identity.

Without altering the scheme of spatial distribution and organization and without touching either the furniture or the floors, Sipek has brilliantly succeeded in radically transforming the perception of the site entrusted to him. And he has done it by putting to optimum use the elements that characterize his own creative language.

Another point of
intervention, the
restrooms, where the
architect has redesigned
all the accessories.
A minimal space, neat
and functional, with
white ceramic tile and
ocher walls.

The key to the change
of ambience, two
openwork screens
placed behind the
facade, on either side
of the entrance, isolate
the restaurant from
the street yet allow
light to penetrate.

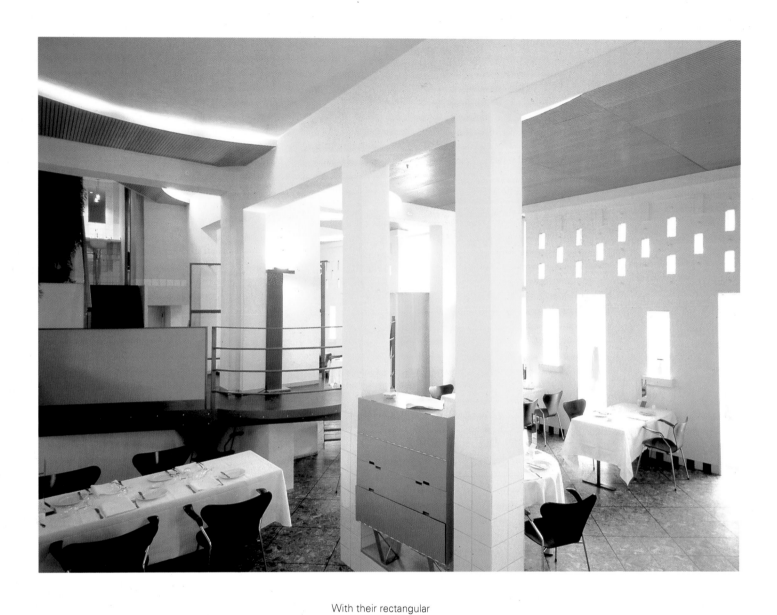

With their rectangular openings in the form of narrow slits or small windows (reminiscent of oriental *moucharabia*) the two screens compose an inner facade of luminous yellow which, along with the false wooden ceiling, give a southern tone to what used to be a cold space.

Jordan Mozer
Iridium
New York, United States

On West 63rd Street in Manhattan, broad plate glass windows offer a glimpse of an organic orange landscape.

A small chest of drawers seems to sway in the background. In front of it a railing rests on a pirouetting ballerina.

Opposite:
The ground floor dining room.
In the foreground a plaster-coated supporting pillar soars toward the undulating ceiling. The indirect lighting emerges from hidden clefts.

Bars, restaurants and assorted venues of urban night life come and go, especially on the fickle New York scene. A particular spot or a whole neighborhood will suddenly find itself propelled into the eye of the media—sometimes only as a shooting star and sometimes as a more lasting light in the Manhattan constellation. Over the past few decades the general movement has been southward: from the Village to Soho, from Soho to Tribeca and from the East Side to the West Side. Abandoned factory and warehouse space has been turned into shops, cafes and restaurants, all uniformly simple and chic, favoring exposed brick walls and well-scrubbed cast-iron columns.

Iridium is from another galaxy. It is of another time and space. Its location, near Central Park and opposite Lincoln Center, makes it out of bounds for the bands of night owls with their well-established habits. And its look is decidedly neither post hi-tech nor trendy minimalist. Iridium takes its inspiration from the organic fantasy-like architecture whose precursors were Gaudi and Mendelsohn. An architecture where the straight line is banished, where the curved edges and surfaces seem to defy the laws of gravity, in a joyous jumble of shapes and colors.

Jordan Mozer says he took his cue from the proximity of Lincoln Center, choosing his themes from the world of music and dance. Yet despite the appearance of unbridled fantasy,

Sketch of three sideboards with expressionistic deformations.

The entrance, drawn to show the deliberate expansion and deformation of volumes.

In this drawing of the buffets, each piece of furniture takes on the aura of a human figure.

Plan of the upper level.

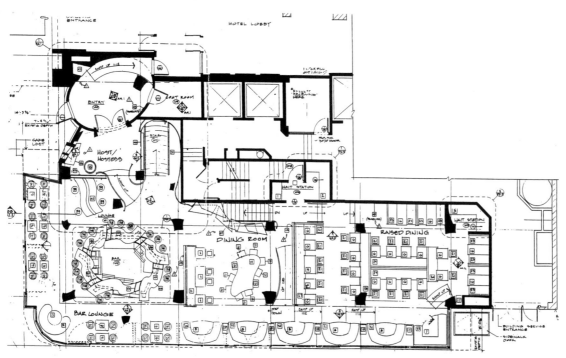

The entrance: a lively expressionistic note.

Overall view of the dining room: no form is repeated as Iridium seeks to be a global work of art, diverse in all its aspects. In the foreground, sofas covered with fabric in Matisse's "Jazz" motif.

The bar flanked by two
oversized columns.
The functional elements
are fully integrated: in the
upper left an air
conditioning vent, at the
back a television screen
embedded in a curving
shaft above the bar.

The ceiling with its broken
volumes and warm colors.
Small luminous sculptures
are decorated with colored
glass. Integrated light
sources and sprinklers
are also raised to the status
of decorations.

this composition meets all the specifications: its layout, from the entrance at the corner of the building to the different areas assigned to the bar, the seating space and traffic paths, is as functional as could be wished. The air conditioning and lighting are perfectly discreet. The entire restaurant, from flooring to furniture, has been put together with meticulous care. The architect used full-scale models and also worked directly with the craftsmen in their workshops, checking the quality of every element and making sure that they would function together. It is not surprising therefore to see how well it all works, conceived as it was to be complex, even convoluted, yet always natural in feel. Worthy of note are the floor, a multicolored mosaic of broken ceramic (as in Barcelona's Parque Guell), light fixtures of colored glass in the tradition of Bruce Goff and chairs reminiscent of Mollin. Each element finds its place in the whole to give an impression of some sort of enchanted grotto. For Mozer, it is in the spirit of Bizet's "Carmen" or Tchaikowski's "Nutcracker Suite." We might add that it evokes a "Cabinet of Doctor Caligari," made by some latter-day Expressionist, imbued with technicolor and musical comedy. A favorite after-theater rendezvous, Iridium has become a high spot on the New York jazz scene—the orange-hued spirals on its walls blend well with the syncopated music.

The dining room, separated from the street by heavy curtains.

Opposite:
A corner of the massive wood bar with its softly flowing lines. The legs of the stools resemble the hooves of animals... or perhaps of satyrs.

A small table lamp: carnivorous plant or fantasy animal?

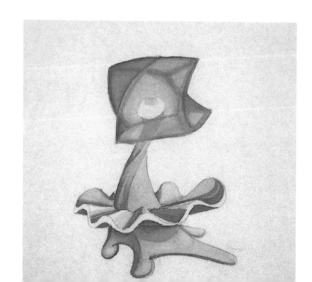

Josep Lluís Garcia
Muffins
Barcelona, Spain

Opposite:
The only apparent concession to modern trends is the treatment of the three pillars, whose original shape was remodeled and covered with satin-finish steel. They attract the eye, but also serve to hold the wooden panels that separate the dining spaces.

Sobriety in the lettering, translucent glass panes in a Japanese style, carefully directed light, the entrance announces a "classic modern" register of restrained elegance.

Anyone walking into a restaurant called Muffins would be entitled to expect a fast-food breakfast place serving donuts and sandwiches and various forms of the speciality featured in the title. But he couldn't be more wrong.

Muffins of Barcelona is a real restaurant, as far-removed in style from the extravagance of modern Catalan *Interiorismo* as it is from the folksy quaintness of those who try to recreate the traditional Spanish inn. The tone of the place is clear even before you enter. The entrance is set back slightly from the street, the facade with its small square panes of translucent glass has a Japanese aura, the whole effect both modern and discreet. Its well-mannered elegance seems bound to attract a young, upwardly-mobile clientele that cares about the quality of the food as much as the beauty of the setting.

The design is the work of architect Josep Lluis Garcia. The space he had to contend with was of medium width but great depth and interrupted by two rows of supporting pillars.

He placed a waiting area and a small bar directly at the entrance and spread out the restaurant over three areas, the first one giving access to the other two by means of a staircase with one flight leading upstairs, the other down.

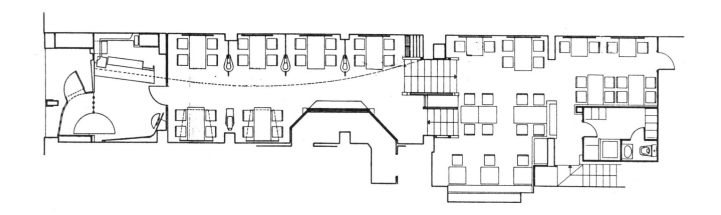

Plan of ground floor
and first floor.

Plan of lower level.

Longitudinal
cross-section clearly
showing the threefold
distribution.

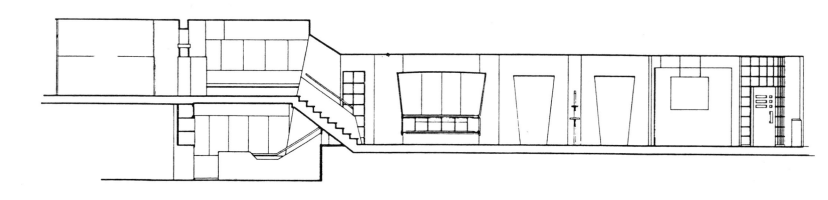

136 Muffins, Barcelona, Spain

The decor is discreet and subtle, and the only concession to modernist taste is to have dressed up the pillars to look like large metal turbine casings. But even this is used to good advantage, for in these casings the architect has inserted wooden panels that act as table separators. The box-like areas thus formed are cleverly set off by the lighting—cone-shaped suspension lamps of minimalist design hang directly over the tables and, from another angle, coming out of the trapezoidal wooden panel, small spots cast a more indirect light.

The staircase connecting the three rooms is a focal point of the restaurant. The architect has treated it with special care—steps of polished granite, a handrail of stainless steel on a thick wood base, shiny metal balcony railings.

The furniture—chairs and tables of plain wood—has the same understated elegance. A large sideboard covered with dark granite holds a selection of hors d'oeuvres displayed for the benefit of the guests.

Lacquered metal stands made of a single folded sheet are the last detail of a classic design that does not bow to passing trends. Such extreme understatement in the decor would seem to be a sign that the owner and architect put great faith in the talents of their chef.

Over a long sideboard of black granite, a mirror gives extra width to a relatively narrow space.

A master stroke, graduated lighting both subtle and precise: indirect light from behind trapezoidal wood panels that anchor each table in its own space, directional from a spot attached high up on the polished wood and, closer to the faces, a halo of soft light from a conical suspension.

138 Muffins, Barcelona, Spain

In general the furniture
is perfectly discreet.
Here and here, several pieces
with strong geometric lines
stand out—a side table
for holding condiments,
a purely decorative little stand
folded from a single sheet
of lacquered metal.

Opposite:
In the downstairs room
the perforated metal covering
of the false ceiling makes it
possible to rearrange the light
suspensions depending on the
layout of the tables.

Key to the three-part distribution, the staircase is treated
with particular care—steps of gray granite inlaid with wood, stainless steel
handrail and shiny metal railings.

Opposite:
The chrome railing on the upper floor takes on copper reflections
from the salmon pink walls.

Thick wooden panels frame the staircase from top to bottom. The architect has
managed to make a decorative space of the slanted wall under the staircase.

Belgo Centraal
London, Great Britain

The access to the restaurant: a metal footbridge embedded with circles of light. On the left, a view downward on the kitchen.

In sharp contrast to the somber brick facade of a former beer warehouse, the brightly-colored sign on the side of the building that proclaims Belgo Centraal is anticonformist and outrageously modern.

Mussels and chips and beer by the gallon may not be the only thing Belgians eat when they're at home, but ever since the idea was exported, it has become the standard fare of the "typical" Belgian restaurant abroad. This simple and traditional formula would certainly have been applied to a new restaurant with the eloquent name Belgo that was about to open in London in the early 1990s. Most probably, the decor would have mattered little—some old tiles and brass fittings would have done the job. It would have been crowded and noisy, with all the hearty good cheer of a Flemish carnival celebration. But by chance (and with the help of Belgo's developer) things worked out quite differently. The location chosen happened to be in Chalk Farm Road, a district of North London that was populated by a new crowd of neo-punk bohemians. And Ron Arad had just opened his new studio One Off a few steps away from the site of the future restaurant. As a neighbor (and willing accomplice) he was invited to do the interior design of the first Belgo, one room of which was, however, given to a more staid and classical designer. The

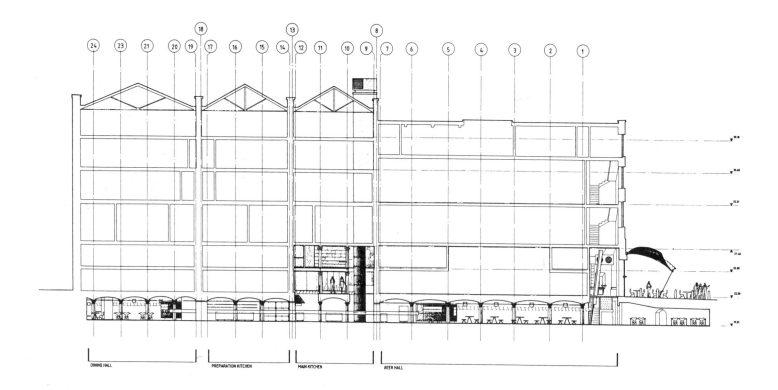

DINING HALL   PREPARATION KITCHEN   MAIN KITCHEN   BEER HALL

Section and plan

of the basement level.

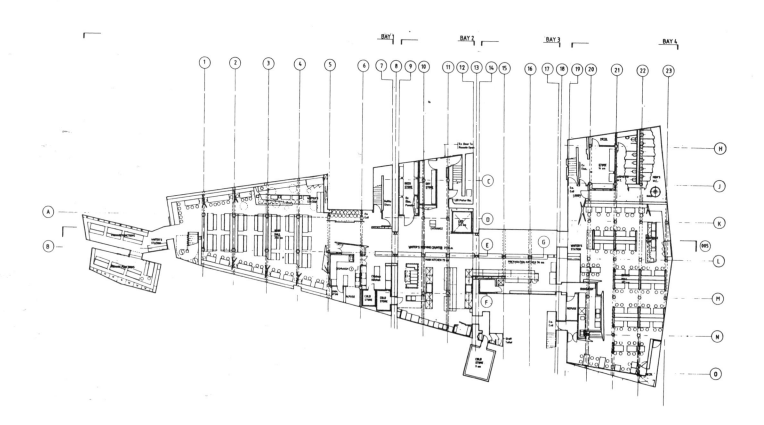

The gleaming red
of the facade makes
the acid pastels of
the entrance look
even more mysterious
by comparison.

This sketch of the
access via the
footbridge accentuates
the desired effect:
a tunnel perspective
emphasized by the
pillars and circles of
light.

Detail of one of the
arcades near the
entrance, done in red
laquered brick.

enormous success of this first undertaking has given rise to a new venue, Belgo Centraal, located in Covent Garden, the old market of central London, reborn as a shopping/dining/leisure complex. Belgo Centraal occupies the entire basement area of a 19th century brick building that used to be a beer warehouse as well as a transversal space between the two streets on the ground and first floor. The building is trapezoidal in shape, with a small courtyard at its broader end.

The plan is broken up into one part for the bar and another for the restaurant and its kitchen. Ron Arad has disposed them in a simple and efficient manner. The bar occupies a slightly vaulted space at the front of the building, in which Arad has highlighted the original cast-iron structure, the beams and columns of which 19th century industrial design had the secret. He furnished it with long tables and benches of bent aluminum sheeting in the spirit of Jean Prouvé's furniture, a heritage that Arad proclaims as part of his work. The restaurant is under the courtyard, which Arad has opened up and covered with a curved glass roof supported by a laminated wood structure whose shape is reminiscent of the inside of a whale.

Here the furnishings are all in supple curves—bean-shaped tabletops and chairs made of a single sheet of molded wood on a metal base.

Just as in the first Belgo, the show begins as soon as you walk through the front door and step onto a metal gangway illuminated from below through circular cutouts. As they enter, the customers can look into the kitchen down below, which is treated in the manner of a ship's engine room. They can see the shine of polished steel, hear the clatter of utensils, watch the cooks and their helpers busy at their work—all of this under dramatic lighting with strange-looking pipes and aeration ducts of shiny steel in twisted shapes. It is a vision both hygienic and reassuring, noisy and stimulating, very appropriate to whet the appetite.

In the basement bar, a good rapport between the beams
and columns of the old structure and the sheet aluminum benches
folded in the manner of Jean Prouvé.

Chair or swimming seahorse? The restaurant chairs have a metal
base, back and bottom made of a single sheet of molded wood.

The restaurant: under an open courtyard, an interior
like the belly of a whale is bathed in natural light. The organic
accents of the furniture give it a look of undersea animals.

The spinal column
of the whale that
supports the glass
roofing is made of
laminated wood inside,
steel outside.

Pilar Líbano

Little Italy

Barcelona, Spain

Opposite:

At the foot of the Ramblas, on the shore of the old port now given over to leisure activities, Spain pays tribute to Italy, the sea, and... to Manhattan. A long terrace stretched out like the deck of an ocean liner.

Pasta as a decorative element of the tables, and color as a theme.

Until the mid-1980s Barcelona was, paradoxically, a port city that offered its inhabitants a rather poor access to the sea. An assertive policy of urban rehabilitation and the coming of the 1992 Summer Olympics brought an end to this state of affairs. The uninspiring shorefront of Barceloneta has now been replaced with a broad promenade and a well-frequented marina. The old port, whose commercial activity has moved further south, has been completely redone in the form of a vast complex: Maremagnum. Designed by architects Viaplana and Pinon, it houses cinemas, shops and restaurants, and its popularity is a sure sign of success. People flock here at all hours to buy electronic gadgets or Barça football shirts and to eat at the multitude of restaurants, which are doing a booming business.

As the competition is fierce, each establishment makes an effort to stand out, either by its cooking or by a strong and easily identifiable image. Little Italy is the name chosen by one of the restaurants in the complex. The designer, Pilar Libano, has created an original ambience by playing on several registers. Situated on the upper level of the complex, the restaurant has a fine terrace overlooking the city. Here the architect has used simple maritime connotations inspired by the immediate environment—the port and the yachts that

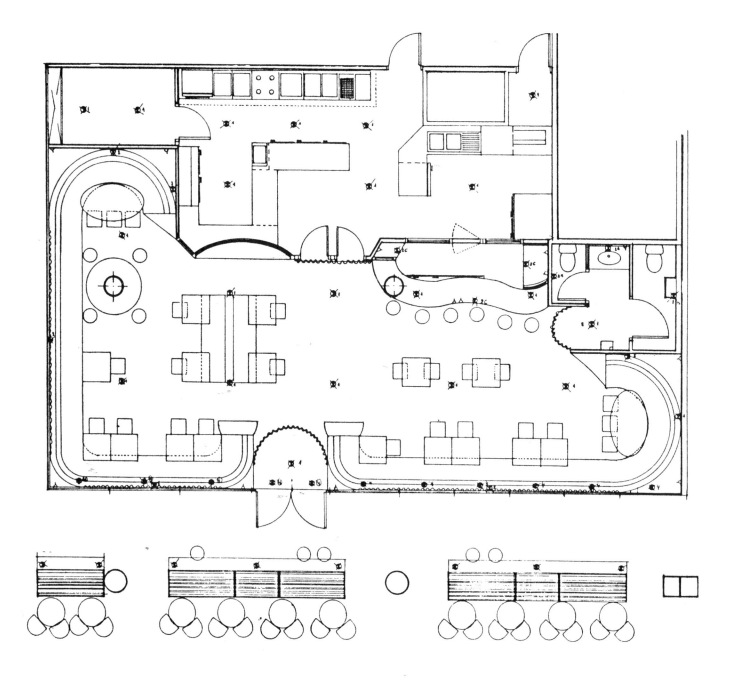

Plan of the restaurant
and the terrace.

Opposite:
The long bench in imitation
leather follows the contour of
the room and assigns each
table its territory by marking
them off in contrasting colors.

Teak wood, chrome pillars, sharp
neat lines, the terrace seems
about to set sail into the night.

154 Little Italy, Barcelona, Spain

are berthed there: the rough wood of the decks, polished wood of the furniture and simple slatted wood backs used for the chairs on the terrace.

The name Little Italy is used with a double twist. First, it announces the kind of food to be served, a statement echoed with some irony by the tabletops, decorated with pasta of various shapes and colors—penne, fusilli, tagliatelle—sprinkled on the table and covered with a plain glass slab.

But Little Italy is also a famous old quarter of downtown New York, near the arty neighborhood of Soho. Here the architect has tried to reconstitute the look of the 1940s American diner. The long, curving bar is dimly-lit and highlighted with chrome. Flush against the wall and running around the entire restaurant is a continuous bench, padded like the booths in the old diners and covered with imitation leather in a range of bright acid colors. Rounded at all the corners, it is divided into different-colored segments to mark off the area of each table. The whole effect is gently nostalgic and lovers of road movies and highway coffee shops will feel right at home. For a final touch, the architect has chosen to add some assorted, unmatched chairs that look as if they had been picked up from flea market here, a garage sale there...

A last bit of irony comes from the outside, from the surrounding landscape. Was it pure coincidence? Or was the architect aware of its presence? In the view from the terrace, the one figure that stands out clearly from the panorama of Barcelona's harbor—the tall solitary figure of Christopher Columbus. He stands on his column at the foot of the Ramblas and points an imperious finger westward, towards the New World... in the direction perhaps of New York... or Little Italy...

Under glass on the teak tabletops, pasta in a variety of shapes and colors.

A maritime look, streamlined profiles, bright colors. A thick column completely covered in wood has a wrap-around rack and service table, like a pair of hula hoops.

Opposite:
The bar sways in an elegant curve accented by satin chrome and caressed by a wooden rail.

A major chord: from atop his
column, Christopher Columbus
points westward to the setting
sun... and to far-off Manhattan.

Opposite:
Rigor and well-tempered
fantasy—the gracefully
unmatched chairs add a touch
of individualism.

Architects' biographies

FIRM: ALLIES AND MORRISON

ALLIES, BOB

Born in 1953.
Graduated from the University
of Edinburgh in 1977.
Awarded Edinburgh Architectural
Association Bronze Medal in 1976.
Visiting Professor at the University
of Edinburgh in 1995, then at the
University of Bath.
Founded firm with Graham Morrison
in 1983, after winning competition to
redesign The Mound in Edinburgh.

MORRISON, GRAHAM

Born in 1951 at Kilmarnock, Scotland.
Graduated from Cambridge University
(1976).
Royal Fine Art commissioner since 11/1997.

MAXWELL, ROBERT

Born in 1957.
Studied at Architectural Association
and London School of Architecture.
Associate member of Allies and Morrison
in 1991.

Principal realizations: British Embassy
in Dublin, redesign of a public space
at Pierhead, Liverpool, business center
in Sheffield, The People's Palace
restaurant at the Royal Festival Hall
and a new gallery for the Contemporary
Applied Arts Gallery in London, Abbey
Mills pumping station on the Thames.

ARAD, RON

Born in 1951 in Tel Aviv.
Studied at the Jerusalem Academy of Art
(1971-1973), then at the Architectural
Association of London (1974-1979).
Based in London since 1973.
In 1981, with Caroline Thorman, created
the One Off studio of conception/design,
manufacture and distribution at Covent
Garden.
In 1989, founded, also with Caroline
Thorman, Ron Arad Associates, Chalk
Farm, London, into which One Off was
integrated in 1993.
In 1994, set up the Ron Arad Studio
in Como, Italy, a studio exclusively for
the production of limited series.
Visiting Professor at the Hochschule
of Vienna (1994-1997) and taught design
at the RCA, London.
Directed a number of design workshops
for students: at the Vitra Design
Museum at Weil am Rhein, Germany, at
Vitra Farm in France and in Ravenna, Italy.
Named Designer of the year in 1994.

Principal realizations:
Furniture and design: Well-Tempered
Chair (1986) and Schizzo Chair (1994) for
Vitra International (Switzerland); chairs
Misfits (1993) and Sof-Sof (1995) for
Moroso (Italy); office accessories (1991)
for Lippert Wilkins (Allemagne); furniture
Anonymous (1994) for Noto (Italy); Empty
Chair and table Fly Ply for Driade (1993);
lighting (1996) for Artemide (Italy);
chairs Fantastic Plastic Elastic (1996-1997)
for Kartell (Italy); CD storage systems
(1997) for Alessi...
Architecture: boutique Bazaar for
Jean-Paul Gaultier in London (1984);

showrooms One Off in Covent Garden
(1983-1986); fashion shops Milano
Monamour in Milan, Equation in Bristol,
Camomilla in Rome; publishing house at,
Black Forest (1993); shop Michelle Mabel
in Milan (1994); bar and restaurant Belgo
in London (1994); foyer for new Tel Aviv
Opera House (1994); office building "Y"
in Seoul (1995), restaurant Belgo Centraal
in London (1995); art gallery Achenbach
in Dusseldorf (1995); Adidas Stadium
in Paris (1995-1996); café-restaurant
Adidas/Kronenbourg in Toulon (1997);
private residence in London (1997).

**ARRIBAS ALFREDO ARQUITECTOS
ASOCIADOS**

ARRIBAS, ALFREDO

Born in 1954 in Barcelona.
Graduated from the Barcelona University
School of Architecture in 1977.
In 1986 founded the firm Alfredo Arribas
Arquitectos Asociados (AAAA), with
Miguel Morte.
Taught at ETSAB from1978 to1990 and
in 1995-1996.
Headed the interior architecture department
at the Elisava school (1979-1989).
Vice-president of FAD (Fomentos de Artes
Decorativas) from 1986 to1988;
president of INFAD (interior architecture
section of FAD) from1982 to1985.
Various prizes and distinctions in Spain
and Japan: Japan Commercial Space
Design Award, Good Design Lighting
Award, in 1994...
Lives and works in Barcelona.

Principal realizations: bars Nandwork
Café (1987) and Torres de Avila (1990)
in Barcelona, nightclub Barna Crossing
in Fukuoka, Japan (1989), Museum
of Contemporary Art Hirai Marugame
in Marugame, Japan (1994). More
recently, in Frankfurt: café Schirn
Kunsthalle, redesigning of Willy Brandt
Platz, hall and buffet-restaurant at central
offices of Commerzbank (with Sir Norman
Foster Office).

BRANSON COATES ARCHITECTURE LTD

COATES, NIGEL

Born in 1949 in Malvern, U.K.
Graduated from Architectural Association
School of Architecture, London, 1974.
Founded his firm in London with Doug
Branson in 1985.
Since 1995 has taught at the Royal
College of Art, London.
Japan Inter-Design award (1990).

Principal realizations: restaurant
Metropole (1985) and café Bongo (1986)
in Tokyo, Jasper Conran stores in London
(1986), Dublin (1987) and Tokyo (1989),
Hotel Otaru Marittimo in Otaru, Japan
(1989), fashion boutiques Jigsaw
in London, Tokyo, Dublin and Manchester
(since 1988), Nishi Azabu building, known
as "The Wall," in Tokyo (1990), nightclub
Taxim in Istanbul (1991), Art Gallery Silo
in Tokyo (1993), bar Bargo in Glasgow
(1996), National Center for Popular Music
in Sheffield (1996-1998).
Design: vases for Simon Moore (1996),
Alessi (1990); aluminum objects for 100%

Design (1995) furniture for Partner and Co
(1997), Poltronova...

GARCIA, JOSEP LLUIS I ANTUNEZ

Born in 1953 in Barcelona.
Graduated from the Barcelona University
School of Architecture (1981).
Founded his firm in Barcelona in 1992.

Principal realizations: boutiques
Simorra in Barcelona and Madrid;
boutique Trazos in Eivissa, veterinary clinic
Tot Cat in Barcelona, restaurant Muffins
in Barcelona, sports complex in St-Cugat,
private houses at Gava, Alella, St-Cugat.

GAVOILLE, KRISTIAN

41 years old.
Architect DPLG, Toulouse (1981).
Collaborator of Philippe Starck from 1986
to1991.
Furniture produced by Disform in Spain
and Neotu in France (1988).
Exhibits regularly at Neotu Gallery, Paris
(1990, 1993, 1996).
Creator of the year at the Salon du meuble
(furniture), Paris, 1992.

Principal realizations:
Architecture: in Paris, designed offices
for France 2 (1992), shop Claude Montana
(1993), company restaurant for Cartier
and restaurant Rusti, Place de la Bastille
(1994), company restaurant Kookai (1995),
café Gavoille in Amiens (1993), store
Marithe & Francois Girbaud in Paris, stores
of the Dooble chain for the company
Celio, design-environment, outlets and
factory for Akteo watches (1997).
Furniture and design: for University
Les Chênes in Cergy-Pontoise (1993),
for Le Mobilier National (1994, 1996);
water bottle for Contrexeville (1994),
parasol for Orangina (1995).
Staging: clips (The Rita Mitsouko, 1990),
set decoratop (Arte, 1994), design of
exhibitions ("La Vitesse" at Foundation
Cartier, 1991, "Variations Gitanes" at
La Villette, 1992), salons Abitare Il Tiempo
in Verona (1992), Salon du Meuble (1994
and 1995) in Paris.

IAVICOLI & ROSSI DESIGN CONSULTANCY

ROSSI, MARIA LUISA

Born in 1958 in Cagliari, Italy.
Graduated from Domus Academy, Milan.
Founded her firm with Vincenzo Iavicoli
in 1985-1986 in Florence: architecture,
design, environmental art, developed mainly
in Japan (Tokyo and Akita).

IAVICOLI, VINCENZO

Born in 1957 in Pescara, Italy.
Graduated from Art Center College of
Design, Pasadena, California (1998).

Principal realizations:
Architecture: store Pete's Collection
and boutique Tesono in Taichung
(Taiwan), boutique Horaya in Fukuoka
(Japan), showroom Modus Vivendi in
Florence, restaurants Nikko and Kabuto
in Tokyo.
Design: mirrors for Nippon Sheet Glass
Co (Tokyo), furniture for Ravarini Castoldi
& Co (Milan), Wakita Hi-Tecs (Fukuoka).

KAITNA, REICHEL, SMETANA

KAITNA, WOLFGANG

Born in Vienna in 1947.
Assistant at Institute of Interior Decoration
and Design (1975-1985) and lecturer
at faculty of architecture (1977-1987)
of the Technical University of Vienna.
Lives and works in Vienna.

SMETANA, KURT

Born in Vienna in 1947.
Architectural studies at the Technical
University of Vienna.
City planner.
Works in Vienna and the region of
Burgenland.

REICHEL, RUEDIGER

Born in 1945 at Bad Ischl, Austria.
Architectural studies at Technical
University of Vienna.
Lives and works in Vienna.
Principal realizations: Kix Bar in Vienna
(1987-1988).

KURAMATA, SHIRO

Born in 1934 in Tokyo, died in 1991.
Graduated from Institute of Design
Kuwasawa (1956).
Founded Kuramata Design Office in 1965.
In 1970, first furniture, Revolving Cabinet.
Mainichi Prize 1972.
In 1981, Kuramata joined the Memphis
group and participated in the exhibition
"Memphis," which traveled to various
American museums, including the MOMA
in New York.
Cultural Design Prize, Japan, 1981.

Principal realizations:
Furniture: bedside lamp Fantome (1972),
commode Marilyn Monroe (1978), side
table Kyoto (1983), chair Begin the Beguine
(1986), chair Ko-Ko (1986), commode
Side 1, Side 2 (1986-1987) chest of drawers
Solaris (1986-1987), armchairs Sing Sing
Sing and How High The Moon (1986-1987),
armchair Miss Blanche (1988), bar stool
BK 86000 (1988-1989)...
Architecture: Lucchino Bar and Caffe Oxy
in Tokyo, shop Esprit in Hong Kong (1986)
Issey Miyake boutiques in Tokyo, Kobe,
New York and Paris (1987), bar Combray
in Shizoka (Japan, 1989), office building
Nara, near Tokyo (1991).

LIBANO, PILAR

Born in Barcelona.
Degrees in interior architecture from
Institutes Iade and Massana, Barcelona
(1978, 1980).
Founded her firm in 1982.

Principal realizations: discotheque
Costa Breve in Barcelona (1990),
discotheque Cibeles in Barcelona (1995),
bar Cel Tibidabo in Barcelona (1994), bar,
restaurant, café Kafka in Barcelona (1997),
restaurant Chiberta in Barcelona (1997)...
Boutiques: Microteam in Barcelona
(1984), Antonio Miro in Barcelona
(1997)...
Interior design: S & C Catalunya
in Barcelona (1991), Fundacion La Caixa
in Barcelona (1992-94)...
Housing decoration.

MARISCAL, JAVIER

Born in 1950 in Valencia, Spain.
Graphic art studies in Barcelona.
Founded his studio, Estudio Mariscal, in 1989.
Image design ("Cobi," mascot for the Olympics in Barcelona 1992, "Twipsy," mascot for Expo Hanover 2000), graphic artist, designer all media, Javier Mariscal has worked for: Akaba, Memphis, Alessi, Swatch, Rosenthal... With Alfredo Arribas: bar Torres de Avila in Barcelona (1990), children's playground Acuarinto in Nagasaki (1992).

Latest realizations: graphic images for the Lighthouse in Glasgow; collections "Hotel 21" for Moroso, and "Pces," bathroom accessories for Cosmic (1997).

MARRONE, ISMAELE

Born in 1954 in Bergamo, Italy.
Graduated from Institute of Architecture at University of Venice in 1980.
Founded his firm in Milan in 1983.

Principal realizations: restructuration of commercial buildings, private houses and apartments in Urgnano (1984), Viadana (1987), Milan (1991)... In Milan, showroom Alivar (1992), restaurant-bar-discotheque La Gare (1993); socio-cultural center in Mozzanica and cemetery Cologno Al Serio in Bergamo (work in progress).

MAYR-KEBER, GERT M.

Born in 1950 in Klagenfurt, Austria.
Graduated from Technical University, Vienna.
From 1974 to1979, worked with Günther Domenig in Graz and Vienna and with Hans Hollein in Vienna.
Founded his firm in Vienna in 1979.
Taught at University of Applied Arts in Vienna (1981-1984), Academy of Visual Arts in Stuttgart (1985-1986), and Technical University of Vienna (1989-1990).

Principal realizations:
In Vienna, Gruenauer apartment (1979), house in Perchtoldsdorf (1981), cafeteria of Fine Arts Museum (1988), houses in Hietzing and Nussdorf (1989), Weiland offices (1989), renovation of offices for Treuhand-Union (1994), neighborhood kindergarten in Oberlaa (1996).

MOZER, JORDAN

Born in 1958 in Chicago.
Studied painting and sculpture at Art Institute of Chicago, literature at University of Wisconsin, industrial and architectural design at University of Illinois.
Founded Jordan Mozer & Associates in 1984, in Chicago.

Principal projects: restaurants Cypress Club in San Francisco (1991), Surf 'n' Turf in Matsuyama (1992), New Wind in Frankfurt (1993), factories H20 Plus and Outer Circle's in Chicago (1994 and 1995), Cheesecake Factory in Chicago (1995). Spectrum Prize for Iridium, New York 1994.

PESCE, GAETANO

Born in 1939 in La Spezia, Italy.
Architectural studies in Venice (1959-1965).

Created his firm in 1962 in Padua.
Signed his first industrial products in 1968, using recycled materials.

Principal realizations:

Design and furniture: armchair Yeti for Cassina (1968-1969), chairs Up for C&B Italy (1969), chairs and armchair Dalila (1980), divan Tramonto a New York for Cassina (1980), tables Sansone I (1980) and Sansone II (1986-1987) for Cassina, Green Street Chair production Vitra International Bale (1984), armchairs Sit Down and I Feltri for Cassina (1986-1987), Umbrella Chair production Zerodisegno (1993-1994), chairs Broadway for Bernini Arredamenti (1992-1995), cabinets Mona Lisa (1991), Anne Franck (1995-1996), Christ Cabinet (1995)...
Architecture: apartment of M. A. Hubin in Paris (1985-1986); residential high-rise in Sao Paulo (1987); Liston bar for hotel Il Palazzo in Fukuoka, Japan (1989) and Organic Building in Osaka (1990); store Dujardin in Brussels (1992-1993); offices of TBWA Chiat/Day in New York (1994).

ROSSI, ALDO

Born in 1931 in Milan, died in 1997.
Graduated from Politecnico of Milan in 1959.
Collaborated from 1955 to 1964 with the publication Casabella Continuita.
In 1966 published L'Architettura della citta.
Taught at University of Palermo (1970), Politecnico de Milan (1972-1973), Polytechnic School of Zurich, as well as at Yale, Harvard, and the Institute for Architecture, New York.
Pritzker Prize in 1990.

Principal realizations: neighborhood housing Gallaratese in Milan (1973), cemetery San Cataldo, with Gianni Braghieri, in Modena (1971), Theatre du Monde in Venice (1979), Rauchstrasse apartments in Berlin (1983), residential buildings for international exhibition Bauaustellung Berlin (1984-1987), Centro Torri in Parme (1985/88), Architecture school for the University of Miami (1986), theater Toronto Lighthouse, with Morris Adjimi in Toronto (1988), hotel Il Palazzo in Fukuoka, Japan (1989).

SIPEK, BOREK

Born in 1949 in Prague.
Graduated from the Technical University of Delft (1979).
Founded his firm in Amsterdam in 1983.
Taught at Academy of Applied Arts in Prague (1990).
Kho Liang le Prize(1989), Prins Berhard Fond (1993).

Individual exhibitions: Museum of Decorative Arts, Lyon (1987), Stedeljik Museum of Amsterdam (1991), Vitra Design Museum in Weil am Rhein, Germany (1992), Museum of Decorative Arts, Prague (1993).
Furniture and objects produced in Italy by Cleto Munari, Driade Spa, and Maletti Spa, in Austria by Leitner and Wittmann, in Switzerland by Vitra, in France by Les Porcelaines de Sèvres and Bernardaud, in Germany by Anthology Quartett and Suessmuth, in the Netherlands by

Alterego, Mosa, and the Steltman Gallery, and in the Czech Republic by Ajeto.
Architecture: Het Kruithuis Museum in Den Bosch, the Netherlands (1993-1998), Kyoto Opera (1994), Karl Lagerfeld boutique in Paris (1995), various homes for individuals in the Netherlands and Germany, 62 apartments in Apeldoorn, the Netherlands (1994-1996), Shoebaloo boutique in Rotterdam (1995), Komatsu facade in Tokyo (1996).

SOTTSASS, ETTORE

Born in 1917 in Innsbruck, Austria.
Graduated from the Polytechnic Institute of Turin (1939).
Created his firm in Milan, in 1947.
In 1957, he took over artistic direction of furniture design, Poltronova; in 1958, started working for Olivetti (creation in 1967 of the typewriter named Valentine...).
In 1981, founded the group Memphis, which he left in 1985.
Created Sottsass Associati in 1981, with Marco Zanini and Mike Ryan.

Principal realizations (aside from design and furniture): low-rent dwellings in Meina, Piemont (1951), ensembles in Carmagnola (1954), home of D. Wolf in Ridgeway, Colorado (1987-1989), Zibibbo bar in the Hotel Il Palazzo in Fukuoka, Japan (1989), extension of the Museum of contemporary furniture in Ravenna (1992-1994).

STARCK, PHILIPPE

Born in 1949 in Paris.
Ecole Nissim-de-Camondo, Paris.
Created Starck Product in 1979.
Taught at the Domus Academy of Milan and the Ecole Nationale des Arts Décoratifs de Paris.
French Grand Prix for industrial creation (1988).

Principal realizations:
Interior architecture: in Paris, La Main Bleue (1976), Les Bains-Douches (1978), café Costes (1984); restaurant Manin and Café Mystique in Tokyo (1986), hotels Royalton and Paramount in New-York (1988 and 1990), restaurants Teatriz in Madrid (1990), Peninsula in Hong Kong (1994), Theatron in Mexico (1995), Asia de Cuba in New York (1997), Hotel Mondrian in Los Angeles (1997).
Architecture: Laguiole knife factory in France (1988), office buildings Nani Nani and Asahi in Tokyo (1989), family homes Catalogue les 3 Suisses, France (1994), Ecole Nationale des Arts Décoratifs (1995) in Paris, Bordeaux airport control tower (1997), waste reprocessing plant in Paris/Vitry (to be completed in 2004).
Design: furniture for the Elysée presidential palace, many furniture pieces and objects produced in France, Italy, Spain, Japan, Switzerland Germany. Industrial design: Beneteau boats, Daum vases, Aprilia scooter, Fluocaril toothbrush, Mikli eyeglasses, Decaux urban furnishings...

TAKASAKI, MASAHARU

Born in 1953 in Kagoshima.
Graduated from Meijo University (1976).
Taught at Stuttgart University and Graz Technology Institute.

Created the Mono Bito Institute in Tokyo in 1982, and the firm Takasaki Masaharu Architects in Kagoshima in 1990.
First prize at the Shinkenchiku Residential Design Competition in 1977.
Best young architect of 1996, Japan Institute of Architects.

Principal realizations: Tamana City Observatory Museum in Kumamoto, Kihokucho Astronomical Museum in Kagoshima, Earth Architecture structure in Tokyo, Restaurant of Asu-Kuju Nature park.

VARIS ARQUITECTES
FREIXES, DANIEL

Born in 1946 in Barcelona.
Graduated from the Barcelona University School of Architecture (1971).
Responsible for exhibitions and conferences of the COAC (Official College of Architects of Catalonia) from 1972 to 1974.
Founded the cooperative Varis Arquitectes in 1976 with Vicente Miranda, later joined by Eulalia Gonzalez and Pep Angli.
Prix FAD 1990 and 1996.

MIRANDA, VICENTE

Born in 1940 in Logrono.
Graduated from the Technical Institute (1963), and the Barcelona University School of Architecture (1973).

Principal realizations: in Barcelona, Clot Park (1982), Cocktail bars (1982), Zsa Zsa (1988) and Seltz (1992), Gaig restaurant (1990), Communication Sciences faculty of the University of Ramon Llull (1995-1996), Magic Barca restaurant for the Barcelona Football Club; in Figueras, exhibition hall of the Dali Foundation (1992-93); in Aragon, renovation of the motorway restaurant (1995).

WINDBICHLER, IRMFRIED

Born in 1947 in Kitzbuehel, Austria.
Graduated from the Graz Technical University (1975).
Created his firm in1982 in Graz.

Principal realizations: in Graz, musical bar Nachtexpress (1990), Spitz magazine (1992), Anna Children's Hospital (1994), garage for Schneider car collection (1997), Kars home at Lule, Portugal (1994), Hotel Linde at Maria Woerth, Austria (1996).

Bibliography

Gail Bellamy, *More Bars, Discos and Nightclubs*, PBC International, Inc., New York, 1995.
Marie-France Boyer, *Le Goût des cafés. Le génie du lieu,* Thames & Hudson, Paris, 1994.
Carlo Branzaglia, *Discodesign in Italia,* under the direction of Silvio San Pietro, Edizioni L'Archivolto, Milan, 1996.
Virginia Croft, *Recycled as Restaurants. Case Studies in Adaptive Reuse,* Whitney Library of Design, Watson-Guptill Publications, New York, 1991.
Martin E. Dorf, *Restaurants That Work. Case Studies of the Best in the Industry,* Whitney Library of Design, Watson-Guptill Publications, New York, 1992.
Roger Gain, *Les Plus Beaux Restaurants de Paris,* Gallimard, Paris, 1989.
Martin M. Pegler, *Theme Restaurant Design. Entertainment & Fun in Dining,* Retail Reporting Corp., New York, 1997.
Collectives works:
Storefront 2. Pubs & Restaurants, Japanese/English bilingual edition, Graphic-sha Publishing Co., Tokyo, 1995.
World Restaurant Designs, 51 Outstanding Ethnic Restaurants, Japanese/English bilingual edition, Shotenkenchiku-Sha Co., Tokyo, 1994.
Japanese Restaurants & Taverns, 51 Outstanding Japanese Specialty Dish Restaurants & Taverns, Japanese/English bilingual edition, Shotenkenchiku-Sha Co., Tokyo, 1996.
Elements of *Showcase of Interior Design,* Vitae Publishing, Inc., Grand Rapids, MI, USA, 1992, and of Wayne Hunt, *Urban Entertainment Graphics.*
Signage and Graphics for Theme Parks, Zoos and Aquariums, Sports, Casinos and Restaurants, Madison Square Press, New York, 1997.
Two special issues, Spanish/English bilingual edition, of *Casas Internacional* :
Guillermo Raul Kliczkowski, Javier Penacca Perez, Diana Veglo, Andrea Birgin, *Bars & Restaurants,* Kliczkowski Publisher-Asppan CP67, Madrid, June 1997.
Hugo Montanaro, Nilda Mutti, *Bars & Restaurants,* Kliczkowski Publisher-Asppan CP67, Madrid, October 1997.

Monographs

Guidot R. and Boissière O., *Ron Arad,* Editions Dis Voir, 1998.
Ernst Wasmuth Verlag, *Alfredo Arribas Architecture and Design works 1991-1995,* Tuebingen, Berlin, 1995.
Rick Poynor, *Nigel Coates : The City in Motion,* Fourth Estate, Londres, 1989.
Anthony Fawcett, *New British Interiors : Nigel Coates-Zaha Hadid,* Art Random, Tokyo, 1991.
Ph. Louguet, *Kristian Gavoille,* Editions du Regard, Paris.
Mariscal Design, Taschen, 1991.
Mariscal 1& 2, NHK, 1992.
Gaetano Pesce, *Le Temps des questions,* Ed.itions du Centre Pompidou, Paris, 1996.
Rossi Aldo, *L'Architettura della citta,* Padoue, 1966, *L'Architecture de la ville,* Paris, 1981.
Braghieri Gianni, *Aldo Rossi,* Bologna, 1985.
Adjimi Morris, *Aldo Rossi : Architecture 1981-1991,* New York, 1991.
Radice B., *Ettore Sottsass,* New York, Rizzoli, Electa, 1993.
De Bure Gilles, *Ettore Sottsass Jr,* Rivages, 1987.
Mnam/CCI, *Ettore Sottsass,* Centre National Georges Pompidou, 1994.
Starck, Taschen, 1991.
Christine Colin, *Starck,* Pierre Mardaga éditeur, Liège.
Franco Bertoni, *Philippe Starck, L'architecture,* Pierre Mardaga éditeur, Liège, 1994.
Starck, Taschen, 1997.

Photo credits

Printed in Italy